PASTA AND RICE

VOGUE

COOKERY COLLECTION

PASTA
AND RICE

HAMLYN

First published in 1988 by
The Hamlyn Publishing Group
Michelin House, 81 Fulham Road
London SW3 6RB

ISBN 0 600 55845 2

Printed in Hong Kong

Text and photographs supplied by Vogue Australia

Vogue Australia Editor-in-Chief **June McCallum**
Vogue Entertaining Guide Editor **Carolyn Lockhart**
Food Editor **Joan Campbell**

Vogue Australia would like to thank the following for their invaluable contribution:

Margaret Agostini (Baby Spinach Ravioli 36, Lobster Ravioli with Truffles 42); Le Bel Age, Los Angeles (Stuffed White Cabbage with Meat and Rice 71); Blaxlands Restaurant, Hunter Valley (Spinach Fettuccine with Smoked Salmon 57); Lydia Bonnin (Pasta with Spinach and Beetroot Leaves 35); Fiorella de Boos Smith (Risotto al Frutti di Mare 85); Diana Bowden (Simple Fried Rice 27); Margie Bromilow and John Stevenson (Gnocchi with Prosciutto and Broad Beans 62, Lobster Medallion on Noodles with Ginger and Coriander Butter 77); Bridget Buckworth (Sushi 44); Joan Campbell (Walnut Sauce 17, Quick Tomato Sauce 21, Fettuccine with Four Cheeses 25, Individual Mushroom Ravioli 36, Green and White Noodles with Mushrooms and Parsley 38, Spaghetti with Courgettes 38, Bow Tie Pasta Primavera 53, Frittata di Spaghetti 55, Lasagne 59, Poussins with Rice and Mushroom Filling 67, Seafood Cannelloni 74); Joan Campbell for THE AUSTRALIAN MEAT AND LIVE-STOCK CORPORATION'S promotions in *Vogue Entertaining Guides* (Indonesian Rice 32, Tomato Fettuccine with Lamb's Liver 60-1, Son-in-Law Eggs 92, Stir-fried Thai Noodles 92, Curry Steamed Rice with Cucumber Relish 92, Thai Muslim Curry 93, Armenian Lamb 94, Rice Pilaf 94); Trish and Julian Canny (Risotto con Melone 64); Francesco Cinzano (Risotto al Brut 28); Franca Corino (Chicken Liver Sauce 25); Manuela Darling (Rotolo di Spinaci 56-7); Shenth Fernando (Sri Lankan Salad 31); Belinda Franks (Pasta Salad with Aubergine and Basil 35); Max Fulcher (Nasi Lemak 86, Prawn Stir-fry 86, Malaysian Curried Chicken 86); Prue Fyfe (Watercress Pasta with Mussels in Wine 58); Jean Gardner (Prawns with Brown Rice 68); Anne Garrett (Pasta con la Ricotta 37); Margot Grace (Fettuccine with Lobster Sauce 74); Sue Gray (Buckwheat Pasta Salad 81); Suelyn Grey (Oriental Rice 66, Quick-fried Bean Sprouts and Water Chestnuts 66); Consuelo Guinness (Arroz Verde 27, Tomato Pasta Salad 54); John and Kay Hansen (Breast of Chicken Avocado 90-1, Wild Rice Irene 91); Lyn Hatton (Spiced Almond Chicken 88, Spinach Rice 88-9, Garam Masala 89, Cucumber Raita 89); Romilly Hobbs (Wild Rice Pilaf 33); Susan Leahy (Koulibiac 67); Carolyn Lockhart (Mushroom and Tomato Sauce 21, Shell Pasta with Prawns and Mange Tout 40, Pasta with Creamy Herb Sauce 54, Paella 84); Pat Lord (Special Tomato Sauce 19); Jean-Luc Lundy (Ravioli of Duck with Asparagus and Watercress Sauce 78); Stefano Manfredi, The Restaurant, Sydney (Tagliatelle with Roasted Pine Nuts 38); Bill Marchetti (Insalata di Tortel-

lini 36-7); Michael McCarty of Michael's Restaurant, Santa Monica (Red Pepper Pasta with Lobster and Basil 42, Goat Cheese Pasta 57); Sandra and Bruce McLean (Ham, Cream and Mushroom Sauce 25); Kerry McManus (Gorgonzola, Pistachio and Cognac Sauce 17); Bobby McNee (Seafood Sauce 22); Fedor Mediansky (Saffron Rice 31); Sandy Michell (Fresh Herb Pasta 11); Lynne Mullins (Risotto Tricolore 28); Paola Murgia (Pasticcio di Maccheroni alla Ferrarese 63); Elise Pascoe (Spinach Tortellini with Chilli Sauce 59, Poppy Seed Tagliatelle with Rabbit, Apple and Fresh Chervil 82, Venison Chestnut Lasagne 82-3); Elise Pascoe and Tullio Calvetti (Orange Fettuccine with Scallops 40); Elise Pascoe and John Kelly (Breast of Quail on Wild Rice 51); Vicky Peterson (Brown Rice with Fresh Herb Sauce 44); Cris dos Remedios (Pork and Crab Porcupine Balls 48, Chilli Sauce 48); Rupert Ridgeway (Javanese Chicken 69, Turmeric Rice 69); Marisa Sillitto (Broccoli Sauce 17); Layla Sorfie and Helen Hutcherson, The Store Charcuterie, Sydney (Wild Rice Salad with Walnut Dressing 47); Deane Stahmann (Mushroom and Pecan Brown Rice Salad 64); Anne Taylor, Taylor's Restaurant, Sydney (Courgette Cream Sauce with Basil and Prawns 21); Thompson & Morgan (Stuffed Tomatoes with Lemon Sauce 51); Mariella Totaro (Timballo di Riso 70); John Vanderveer, Barrenjoey House, Sydney (Oyster Ravioli with Scallops and Champagne Sauce 76, Warm Pasta Salad with Quail and Abalone 78-9); Judy Villanova (Risotto con Funghi 47).

Our thanks to the following publishers and individuals for permission to reproduce these recipes:

Timbale of Macaroni with Chicken, copyright © Jean Govoni Salvadore. Villa d'Este; Pasta all'Uovo, Spaghetti con Vongole, Fettuccine Alfredo, copyright © Villa d'Este, from *Cooking Ideas from Villa d'Este*, by Jean Govoni Salvadore; Pesto, Spaghetti Neri, Tagliatelle alla Frantoiana, copyright © 1982 by Giuliano Bugialli, *Classic Techniques of Italian Cooking*, Simon & Schuster, 1982; Risi e Bisi, Saffron Pasta, copyright © Giuliano Bugialli, *The Taste of Italy*, Stewart, Tabori & Chang/Conran Octopus, 1984; Spiced Basmati Rice, reproduced from *Madhur Jaffrey's Indian Cookery* by Madhur Jaffrey with the permission of BBC Enterprises Ltd; Meagadarra, copyright © Arabella Boxer; Wild Rice with Shiitake and Onions, Risotto con Porcini, copyright © Elizabeth

Schneider; Nutmeg Noodles with Morels and Cream, copyright © Elizabeth Schneider, *Uncommon Fruits and Vegetables: A Commonsense Guide*, Harper & Row; Steamed Vegetable Rice with Courgettes and Carrots, copyright © Ken Lo, *Healthy Chinese Cooking*, Pan Books Ltd.; Salad of Noodles with Crayfish (originally Yabbies) and Smoked Salmon, copyright © Jean-Jacques Lale-Demoz, *Jean-Jacques Seafood*, Thomas Nelson Australia; Basic Pasta Dough (Oil-free Pasta Dough in this collection), Fettuccine with Prosciutto and Asparagus, copyright © 1984 by Tango Rose, Inc. from *Chez Panisse Pasta, Pizza and Calzone*, by Alice Waters, Patricia Curtan and Martine Labro. Copyright © 1984 by Tango Rose, Inc. Reprinted by permission of Random House, Inc. and Lescher & Lescher; Asparagus Risotto, from *Greene on Greens*, copyright © 1984 by Bert Greene. Reprinted by permission of Workman Publishing. All rights reserved; Rice-stuffed Leeks, copyright © Suzy Benghiat, *Middle Eastern Cookery*, Weidenfeld & Nicolson Ltd; Crab and Basil Ravioli, copyright © Alan Dutournier, The House of Krug presents recipes for La Vie de Champagne (recipe from Restuarant Au Trou Gascon, Paris); Walnut Vinaigrette (in Buckwheat Pasta Salad), from *Salad in Season* by Penny Smith, published by Macmillan, Melbourne 1983.

Grateful thanks to the following photographers:

Richard Bailey 37; Michael Cook 28, 49, 65; Joshua Greene 43; John Hay 16, 24, 62, 89; Franco Pasti 11, 18, 23; Patrick Russell 26; George Seper 2, 6, 30, 39, 40, 45, 46, 50, 53, 55, 56, 58, 63, 66, 68, 70, 72, 75, 77, 79, 81, 83, 84, 85, 87, 91; Rodney Weidland 20, 29, 32, 34, 41, 61, 93, 94.

Publishers' acknowledgments

Special photography (8 and 12) Chris Crofton; *Editor* Wendy Lee; *Contributing Editor* Suzy Powling; *Editorial Assistant* Carolyn Pyrah; *Art Editor* Pedro Prá Lopez; *Designer* Michelle Stamp/Crucial Books; *UK Consultant* Jenni Fleetwood; *Artworks* Tim Mulkern (11), Tony Morris/Linda Rogers Associates (14), Maggie Smith (borders); *Production Controller* Audrey Johnston.

CONTENTS

INTRODUCTION

Staple foods for centuries, rice and pasta have exciting new roles in modern cuisine

Rice and pasta are doubly blessed in that they are both satisfying and enjoyable. And that is probably why they are never really out of fashion. In this *Vogue Cookery Collection* these staple foods are combined with carefully chosen ingredients and flavours in an irresistible collection of recipes.

Indispensable to today's busy cook, these two store-cupboard standbys are the ideal basis for impromptu meals as well as the sensible groundwork for a healthy family nutrition programme, but perhaps their greatest appeal is their versatility.

Pasta comes in an impressive array of shapes and sizes, while sauces to partner it include not only the classic inventions of Italy, but also new and exciting ideas created by its admirers worldwide. And, although rice is inevitably associated with Oriental styles of cooking, as an accompaniment it has an astonishing international talent.

For years pasta and rice have been seen as heavyweight main-course ingredients. Our chapter on first courses, however, offers plenty of fresh thoughts for their place on the starting block. And because of their simplicity of preparation and versatility, they are a blessing for relaxing meals at home. The recipes suggested are frequently ideal for lunches but they would certainly serve equally well at an informal supper.

Neither rice nor pasta should be regarded as a poor relation, however. A combination of superb ingredients and culinary skill has produced an array of dishes that demonstrate, without a doubt, that pasta and rice perform brilliantly at any stylish celebration.

Shell-pink strands of angel's hair, flowing lengths of creamy fettuccine, dusky knots of noodles green and black; pasta may be historically a staple food but it is far from pedestrian. Both its appearance and flavour still excite the imagination of modern cooks, prompting intriguing combinations.

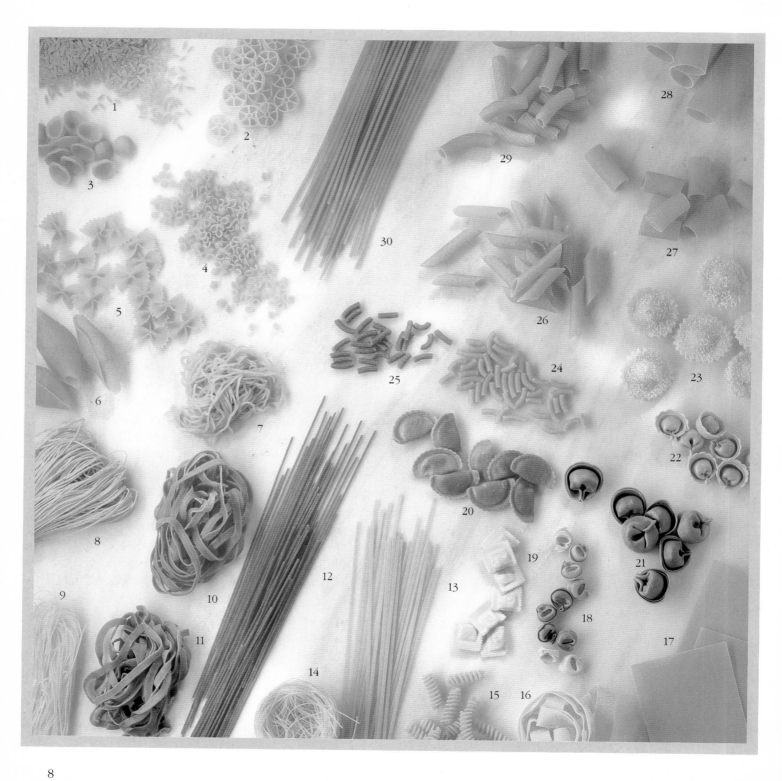

COOKING WITH PASTA

Although the origins of pasta are uncertain, the place it occupies in Italian culinary life has long been established. And when, during the Middle Ages, the tomato began to be cultivated in Europe, the scene was set for a partnership which has flourished for centuries.

Quite simply, pasta means dough, a plain substance made from flour, water and salt. The flour is that milled from durum, or hard, wheat, differing from the wheat cultivated for bread. Pasta is available commercially dried or fresh or may be home-made. The latter requires eggs and a little oil in its making. Commercial pasta – if it contains eggs it will be labelled *all'uovo* – comes in an astonishing range of shapes and sizes. The small delicate types, such as stars or *semini*, are best added to soups for interesting substance. The spaghetti or tagliatelle (noodle) pastas are just as delicious eaten alone, tossed in a little butter or olive oil, as they are with simple sauces. Ribbed rigatoni and other chunky, tubular pastas combine well with more robust sauces, while the more decorative varieties, such as bows and twists, are invaluable for presentation. The filled varieties, such as ravioli, complete the family.

Pasta is not difficult to make at home, but naturally care must be taken and only the best ingredients used. If you make the dough in a food processor, you may prefer to omit the oil and increase the number of eggs.

To cook pasta, use a large quantity of salted water in a very big saucepan so that the pieces can't stick together. Dried pasta will take between 8 and 12 minutes, depending on its size; fresh pasta cooks more quickly, so test soon, even after 1 minute. When it rises to the surface of the boiling water it is ready. All pasta should be *al dente*, or cooked with a little bite to it. Strain it immediately and transfer to a warmed serving bowl deep enough to maintain the heat, with a little olive oil or butter in the bottom. Serve immediately.

PASTA ALL'UOVO

(Basic Egg Pasta Dough)

SERVES 6

350 g/12 oz plain flour
3 large eggs
pinch of salt
1 tablespoon olive oil

TO MAKE DOUGH BY HAND: pour the flour into a mound on the work surface. Make a well in the middle and break in the eggs. Add the salt and the oil. Beat the eggs lightly with a fork to combine them with the oil. Start mixing the flour into the eggs in a circular movement with your fingers. Use one hand for mixing, the other to push flour into the centre. Keep working until you have obtained a well-combined doughy ball. Sprinkle the work surface and your hands with a little flour and start kneading the dough by pushing the pasta away from you until it is quite elastic and does not break off when you pull. Sprinkle the ball of dough with flour and cover it with a damp cloth. Leave it to rest for 1-2 hours in a cool place.
TO ROLL OUT BY HAND: divide the ball of dough into 2 or 3 pieces of manageable size. Sprinkle the cleaned work surface lightly with flour. With a rolling pin, roll out the first piece, then roll and stretch it round the pin about 12 times to thin it out. Sprinkle the dough lightly with flour each time. When it is as thin as a piece of cloth, lay the sheet of pasta on a floured cloth to rest and repeat the rolling and stretching process with the remaining piece(s) of dough. The thickness is governed partly by the kind of pasta you wish to make, but also by the fact that egg pasta swells up when it is cooked.
TO CUT PASTA BY HAND: lightly flour the rolled-out sheet of pasta and cut out the size and shape you want with a sharp knife. If you are making noodles or linguine, roll up the sheet and then cut it carefully in slices of the correct width.
TO MAKE DOUGH IN A FOOD PROCESSOR: increase the amount of flour by 45 g/1½ oz, and add another extra-large egg. If this is too rich a mixture for your taste, substitute up to 2 tablespoons of water for the extra egg, adding it cautiously after the other eggs. The dough must not be too wet.

Fit the metal blade to the machine and place the flour and salt in the bowl. With the machine running, first pour the olive oil through the feed and then add the eggs one by one. Run the machine until the dough comes away cleanly from the side of the bowl. Remove the dough, cover it with a cloth, and leave it to rest for 1-2 hours in a cool place.
TO ROLL OUT IN A PASTA-MAKING MACHINE: divide the ball of dough into 3 pieces and flatten them with your hands. Set the rollers at the widest mark and pass the first piece of dough through. Fold the sheet in three to fit the width of the rollers and roll again. Sprinkle the dough with a little flour if it is too sticky, and fold and roll it again. You will need to do this about 12 times until the piece of dough is smooth and even. At this point you can begin to reduce the width of the roller opening so that the sheet of dough becomes progressively thinner. Reduce by one notch at a time, and do not fold the sheet of pasta between rollings. When you have achieved the thickness you want, place the sheet of pasta on a dry, lightly floured cloth to rest for 15 minutes and repeat the process with the remaining 2 pieces of dough.
TO CUT PASTA BY MACHINE: with a sharp knife cut the sheets of pasta to fit the width of the machine and about 45 cm/18 inches long. Pass each sheet through the cutter, holding the dough with one hand and turning the handle with the other.

PASTA VERDE

(Green Pasta)

Green pasta is made by adding spinach purée to the basic pasta dough. Not only does this change the colour, but it provides a subtle flavour which is more marked in home-made pasta than in commercial varieties. There is also, of course, an added nutritional element.

For the quantities given in the basic recipe above, you will need between 225 and 250 g/8 and 9 oz of fresh spinach leaves (the stalks are too coarse). Wash the spinach thoroughly in cold water and drain it well. Without adding any water, place the leaves in a saucepan over a moderate heat. Cover the pan and cook for about 10 minutes or until the spinach is tender. Drain it very well, squeezing it to extract all the liquid. Chop it very finely, or work it to a purée in a blender or food processor.

Incorporate the spinach purée into the basic recipe at the beginning, placing it in the well of flour, or feeding it into the food processor, with the eggs, salt and oil.

TOMATO PASTA

To make tomato pasta, which is a lovely coral colour, add 1 tablespoon of concentrated tomato purée to the basic recipe, incorporating it at the beginning with the eggs, salt and oil.

This type of pasta is particularly useful for adding colour to a dish, and a mixture of white, green and tomato noodles in a simple sauce of cream and Parmesan cheese is both attractive and appetising.

FRESH HERB PASTA

Fresh herb pasta is so attractive and delicious that it easily serves as a simple lunchtime or supper dish with nothing to accompany it other than a little oil or butter and a scattering of freshly ground black pepper. It combines very well, however, with creamy sauces, fish or chicken if you are planning a more elaborate meal.

To the basic Pasta all'Uovo recipe add 50 g/2 oz of finely chopped mixed fresh herbs of your choice, such as chives, mint, basil, marjoram and parsley, and 1 large clove of garlic, peeled and crushed. If you are making pasta by hand, add the herbs, which must be washed and thoroughly dried on a clean towel, to the flour. Incorporate the garlic with the eggs, salt and oil. If you are using a food processor, first purée the herbs in the machine before adding the flour. Add the crushed garlic at the same time as the eggs.

OIL-FREE PASTA DOUGH

SERVES 6

350 g/12 oz plain flour
a little salt
3 large eggs, beaten
a little water, if necessary

Put the flour in a bowl with the salt and make a well in the centre. Add the eggs and, working with the fingertips, begin to blend the flour and eggs, working from the centre out, gradually gathering flour from the sides. Mix the flour and the eggs, getting the particles next to each other without actually working or kneading the dough. When you have the flour and eggs mixed, add a few drops of water and begin to bring it all together as a mass. Turn it out on to a table

and begin to knead. It will take several minutes to produce a very firm, smooth and strong dough.

The amount of moisture in the dough is the most critical element: this varies according to the size of the eggs and type of flour. As the dough comes together, decide whether a little water is needed, or whether it is too soft and requires a little more flour. Do this at the beginning, because the dough will resist the addition of flour or water after you really begin working it. It is better if the dough is on the dry side, making it necessary to add a few sprinklings of water as you knead, than to try to incorporate more flour into dough that is too soft.

When you have the right amount of moisture in the dough – and experience will teach you what that is – knead the paste for 10-15 minutes then cover it to prevent a dry skin from forming and let it rest for at least 45 minutes before rolling and cutting (see instructions left).

Once rolled out, Oil-free Pasta Dough is as versatile as traditional pasta.

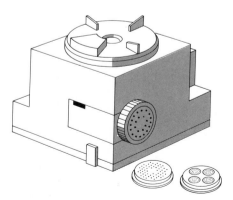

Electric machines transform making pasta into a fully automatic operation.

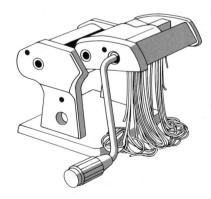

Hand-operated machines cut dough into a variety of lengths and widths.

COOKING WITH RICE

Although rice is inevitably associated with the Far East – after all it was considered a staple crop in China as long ago as 2800 BC – the spread of its cultivation is worldwide. It grows in Africa, Australia and South America, as well as in the United States, the nation which is the world's leading rice exporter. In Europe, rice is grown in Italy and can now be found in both the south of France and in Spain.

No matter where it is grown, rice is a vitally important part of the diet. An excellent source of carbohydrates, it also contains some protein, minerals, a trace of vitamin B and a little fat and fibre. Including it in any menu plan means that it can be given a variety of treatments, limited only by the cook's creativity.

Rice comes in many forms. Most short-grained kinds are used for sweet dishes and do not feature in the following recipes. Leaving them aside, the main rice types to become familiar with are:

LONG-GRAIN RICE: this is usually used for savoury dishes. This rice is milled to remove the outer husk, then pearled or polished to remove the bran and give the grains a sheen.

EASY-COOK RICE: this is long-grain rice which has been steamed under pressure before milling. This process forces the nutrients in the husk and bran more evenly throughout the grain. The result is a rice which is easy to cook, and higher in vitamin content than ordinary long-grain rice.

BASMATI RICE: this is grown in upland areas of India and Pakistan, and on dry land rather than in water. It has a long grain, a distinctively delicious aroma and nutty taste – and about twice the nutrient value of other white long-grain rice.

BROWN RICE: this has the indigestible outer husk removed, but it retains the bran. This results in a higher vitamin content, more fibre and a stronger flavour than white rice. It also takes a little longer to cook than the refined types mentioned here.

SHORT-GRAIN RICE: Arborio is a fine Italian short-grain rice which is especially successful for recipes such as risotto or paella.

WILD RICE: American wild rice is, in fact, an aquatic grass. It has a nutty flavour, is very nutritious and looks attractive. It is, however, difficult to harvest, which means it is more expensive than conventional rice. Cook wild rice in the same way as brown rice.

The rice plant (Oryza sativa), *an erect grass which grows in wet ground, has drooping flower spikes and bears oblong edible grains. Over half the world's population depends on rice as a staple food, and it has been cultivated in India and China for over 5,000 years.*

Because of its long history and its association with so-called exotic recipes, many cooks are wary of rice and go in perpetual quest of a foolproof method of preparing and cooking it.

The main point to remember is that – with the exception of risottos and some Eastern dishes which require 'sticky rice' – savoury rice should have separate and fluffy grains after cooking. There are many ways of achieving this result – try out the methods on page 15 and master one which suits your individual style of cooking.

There are differing thoughts about the need to wash rice before it is cooked. Washing removes excess starch and prevents the grains sticking together. Cooked rice can be rinsed in boiling water to prevent this. Whether you start the rice off in cold or boiling water, it is a good idea to give it a stir before placing the lid on the pan, again to separate the grains. Some cooks, however, maintain that the polishing process leaves the grains so smooth that none of this is really necessary any more.

Discovering a foolproof method of cooking rice is a matter of time and experience. It should not be long before you can begin to experiment with the countless variations that cooks have created for this indispensable food.

PLAIN BOILED RICE

Experiment with the three methods described here to find which suits you best.

METHOD 1

This method is suitable for all types of long-grain rice. The rice is cooked in a volume of water equal to its own, and the rule applies no matter what the size of the measure. Measure the rice before washing it.

SERVES 4-6

2 cups rice
2 cups water
salt, if required

Wash the rice twice in cold water or until the water is clear. Drain well. Place the rice in a heavy-bottomed saucepan and add 2 cups cold water. Bring to the boil over a high heat and let it boil, uncovered, for 2 minutes. Cover the pan tightly and reduce the heat to very low. Do not lift the lid for 15 minutes. At the end of the cooking time the rice will have absorbed all the liquid, while the grains will be fluffy and separate.

METHOD 2

Suitable for all types of long-grain rice, this method resembles the cooking of pasta, in which a large volume of boiling water allows each grain to cook separately.

SERVES 4-6

350 g/12 oz rice
salt to taste

Do not pre-wash the rice. Bring a large saucepan of salted water to the boil. Throw in the rice, let the water come back to the boil and stir it once. Leave the saucepan uncovered and boil for 10 minutes (Basmati rice) or 15 minutes (other long-grain varieties). Drain the cooked rice into a strainer. If the rice is not well separated, pour boiling water through the strainer to rinse it. Drain well.

METHOD 3

Brown rice is best cooked by this method. The volume of water and rice is measured first, as in Method 1, but the proportions differ – for every cup of rice, 2 cups of water are needed – and the rice is added to boiling water rather than cold. When cooking brown rice, don't forget to allow more time than you would for other types of rice.

SERVES 4-6

25 g/1 oz butter
2 cups brown rice
4 cups water
1 teaspoon salt

Melt the butter in a medium, heavy-bottomed saucepan over a low heat. Stir in the rice with a wooden spoon so that all the grains are coated. Add the boiling water and salt. Bring back to the boil, stir once, cover the pan tightly and reduce the heat to very low. Do not lift the lid for 35 minutes. At the end of the cooking time the rice will have absorbed all the liquid, while the grains will be separate, tender and will still remain slightly nutty to the bite.

RISOTTO

Risotto differs from boiled rice in its texture: it should be smooth and creamy, but not sticky or lumpy, and it cannot be left to cook unattended. The rice must be stirred frequently throughout the cooking process to ensure an even result. If you are using a well-flavoured chicken stock, extra seasoning should not be necessary. In Italy, risotto can be a meal in itself, perhaps with the addition of freshly grated Parmesan cheese with the final gloss of butter.

SERVES 4-6

25 g/1 oz butter or 1 tablespoon good
  olive oil
1 medium onion, peeled and chopped
  finely
450 g/1 lb Arborio rice
150 ml/¼ pint dry white wine
1.25 litres/2¼ pints hot chicken stock
  (preferably home-made)
25 g/1 oz butter, to finish

Melt the butter or oil in a heavy-bottomed deep frying pan set over a low heat. Cook the onion gently until it is soft and transparent but not browned. Stir in the rice so that every grain is well coated with butter or oil. Add the wine. Let the rice cook over a moderate heat until almost all the wine has evaporated. With the stock kept hot in a separate saucepan, start adding the stock to the rice 250 ml/8 fl oz at a time, carefully stirring in each addition with a large fork to avoid mashing the rice. If the rice is not cooked after 30 minutes and all the stock has been used, add a little hot water.

When the rice is cooked, quickly fork in the butter and serve.

CHAPTER ONE

SAUCES FOR PASTA

Whether they are traditional favourites or intriguing innovations, these delicious pasta sauces make superb use of the finest ingredients

BROCCOLI SAUCE

SERVES 6

225 g/8 oz broccoli heads
1 tablespoon olive oil
2 small cloves garlic, peeled and chopped
* finely*
salt
freshly ground black pepper

Separate the broccoli into very small florets. Heat the oil in a large frying pan over a moderate heat. Throw in the broccoli and garlic and cook for about 10 minutes, stirring and shaking the pan to prevent the vegetables from sticking. Add salt and freshly ground pepper to taste.

TO SERVE: place 450 g/1 lb freshly cooked pasta, such as fettuccine or pasta shells, in a warmed bowl. Quickly stir in 50 g/2 oz freshly grated Parmesan cheese. Add three-quarters of the broccoli sauce and toss it well to coat the pasta evenly. Turn into individual serving bowls and spoon the remaining sauce on top.

WALNUT SAUCE

SERVES 6

225 g/8 oz walnuts, chopped finely
250 ml/8 fl oz single cream
6 tablespoons freshly grated Parmesan
* cheese*
½ teaspoon dried thyme or 1 teaspoon
* fresh thyme*
salt
freshly ground black pepper
½ teaspoon ground cinnamon

Place all the ingredients in a small heavy saucepan over a low heat. Cook, stirring all the time, until the cheese has melted. Bring the nut and cheese mixture just to the boil and serve immediately.

TO SERVE: the ideal accompaniment is home-made walnut macaroni. To the basic Pasta all'uovo (see page 10) add 50 g/2 oz shelled and crushed walnuts with the flour, and use walnut oil instead of olive oil.

Walnut sauce also goes well with fettuccine, and makes a good partner for cannelloni filled with a mixture of spinach and ricotta cheese.

GORGONZOLA, PISTACHIO AND COGNAC SAUCE

SERVES 4

2 tablespoons shelled pistachio nuts
100 g/4 oz butter
75 g/3 oz Gorgonzola
120 ml/4 fl oz single cream
2 tablespoons cognac, flamed
salt
freshly ground black pepper

Rub the pistachios together to remove as much as possible of the outer skin. Reserving a few whole nuts to use as a garnish, chop the remainder roughly or grind briefly in a food processor.

Place the butter with the cheese in a heavy-bottomed saucepan over a moderate heat. Stir until both have melted and blended together. Add the cream and cook very gently for 5 minutes, stirring.

Remove the pan from the heat and stir in the pistachios and cognac. Season to taste.

TO SERVE: pour the hot sauce over a bowl of freshly cooked small pasta shells (conchigliette) and garnish with pistachios.

Fresh herbs and vegetables offer an infinite variety of combinations for delicious pasta sauces.

PESTO

(Basil Sauce)

This is the classic sauce of Genoa in northern Italy, which the Genoese claim is only at its best made with their basil. Parmigiano is the name given to Parmesan cheese (called *grana* in Italy), by the Parmenese themselves. Pecorino is an Italian cheese made from sheep's milk, while caprino (*capra*) is a creamy mild cheese with a fresh flavour. It is generally sold at Italian delicatessens.

SERVES 4

1 tablespoon pine nuts
1 small clove garlic, peeled
salt
freshly ground black pepper
40 medium basil leaves (about 50 g/2 oz)
2 tablespoons finely grated Parmigiano
2 tablespoons pecorino
2 heaped tablespoons caprino
250 ml/8 fl oz olive oil

Place the pine nuts, garlic, salt and pepper in a stone mortar. Use a wooden pestle, not to crush, but rather to push the ingredients in a circular motion against the stone, which will grind them.
    Add the basil leaves and grind until they are well integrated. Add the Parmigiano, pecorino and caprino and grind the mixture a little more.
    Transfer the mixture to a bowl. Add the olive oil, little by little, mixing with a wooden spoon, until the pesto becomes very creamy and smooth.

Capture the essence of Italy in making Pesto with traditional, top-quality ingredients in the time-honoured way.

TO SERVE: pesto can be served with any pasta. Trenette, the pasta of Genoa, is a kind of square-cut spaghetti which would be particularly appropriate. It may also be served with gnocchi (little dumplings) or stirred into minestrone soup.

SPECIAL TOMATO SAUCE

SERVES 8

15 g/½ oz butter
1 tablespoon olive oil
1 medium onion, peeled and chopped finely
2 cloves garlic, peeled and crushed (optional)
2 Granny Smith apples, peeled , cored and grated
2 medium carrots, peeled and diced finely
2 stalks celery, chopped finely
1 small sweet red pepper, chopped finely
2×425 g/15 oz cans tomatoes, chopped, juice reserved
3 tablespoons tomato purée
1 teaspoon dried oregano
½ teaspoon dried basil
½ teaspoon dried rosemary
freshly ground black pepper

Heat the butter and oil in a large saucepan over a moderate heat. Fry the onion and garlic, if used, until the onion is transparent but not brown. Add all the remaining ingredients and stir well together. Cover the pan and cook for 20-30 minutes over a gentle heat, until the sauce is nicely thickened and a good colour, and the flavours well integrated.
TO SERVE: this sauce is particularly good with tortellini, with freshly grated Parmesan cheese sprinkled over.

SALSA DI SPINACI

(Spinach Sauce)

SERVES 2-4

50 g/2 oz butter
1 onion, peeled and chopped finely
1×227 g/8 oz packet frozen spinach, thawed and well drained
¼ teaspoon ground nutmeg
salt
freshly ground black pepper
150 ml/¼ pint plain yoghurt

Melt the butter in a large saucepan over a moderate heat and fry the onion for 5 minutes until cooked but not browned. Add the spinach and nutmeg. Season to taste and bring to the boil, stirring occasionally. Continue to cook for 5 minutes, still stirring, until the spinach is cooked but still freshly coloured. Reduce the heat, stir in the yoghurt and heat the sauce through.
TO SERVE: add 225 g/8 oz tagliatelle, cooked, drained and tossed with a little butter and freshly ground black pepper, to the spinach sauce. Stir them together briefly over the heat until the pasta is heated through. Transfer to a warmed serving dish and serve at once.

SAUCES TO STORE

Double the quantity of ingredients when preparing basic Italian sauces to use with pasta. Divide the finished sauce into two portions and freeze one for future use.

COURGETTE CREAM SAUCE WITH BASIL AND PRAWNS

As a variation, use freshly grated Parmesan cheese in place of the seafood, adding it with the chopped basil just before serving.

SERVES 4-6

450 g/1 lb baby courgettes, chopped
coarsely (reserve 2 courgettes cut into
julienne or thin diagonal rounds)
65 g/2½ oz butter
1 medium onion, peeled and chopped
325 ml/11 fl oz single cream
salt and freshly ground black pepper
24-30 uncooked prawns, peeled and
cleaned
1 tablespoon freshly chopped basil leaves

Heat half the butter in a frying pan over a moderate heat. Fry the chopped courgettes and onion until lightly coloured. Add the cream. Reduce the heat, cover the pan and cook until the courgettes are softened. Allow to cool a little then purée in a blender or food processor or push through a sieve. Season to taste. Place the mixture in a saucepan, cover and set it in a larger pan of simmering water to keep warm.

Melt the remaining butter in a frying pan over a low heat. Fry the courgette slices and prawns, stirring, until they are almost cooked. (The time will vary depending on size and quantity.) Add the puréed courgettes to the courgette and prawn mixture. TO SERVE: add 450 g/1 lb cooked fettuccine to the sauce. Toss lightly, and transfer to a serving dish. Add the basil and serve.

Mushroom and Tomato Sauce on tagliatelle, made in minutes and irresistibly simple, sums up the appeal of Italian food.

FRESH TOMATO SAUCE

MAKES ABOUT 4×225 G/8 OZ JARS

25 g/1 oz butter
1 large onion, peeled and chopped finely
2 cloves garlic, peeled and crushed
2 rashers streaky bacon (optional),
without rind, chopped
1 large carrot, peeled and grated
1 kg/2 lb ripe, red tomatoes, peeled, seeded
and chopped
120 ml/4 fl oz dry white or red wine
1 bouquet garni
salt
freshly ground black pepper

Heat the butter in a saucepan over a moderate heat and cook the onion, garlic and bacon gently until the onion is soft. Add the remaining ingredients and simmer, partly covered, for 45 minutes, stirring frequently. Add a little water if necessary. The sauce should be thick, but can be thinned as you wish with beef or chicken stock when you use it. Remove the bouquet garni and season to taste.

TO SERVE: tomato sauce is one of the most versatile of Italian sauces, but it is particularly good with a spinach-flavoured pasta, such as green tagliatelle.

QUICK TOMATO SAUCE

SERVES 6

40 g/1½ oz butter
1 medium onion, peeled and chopped
1 large clove garlic, peeled and crushed
a few leaves of fresh oregano
2×425 g/15 oz cans peeled tomatoes,
drained
salt
freshly ground black pepper

Melt the butter in a large saucepan over a moderate heat. Cook the onion until soft and transparent but not brown. Add the garlic, oregano and tomatoes. Season to taste. Cover the pan and cook gently until the onion is cooked and the flavours well combined. Purée the sauce in a liquidizer and strain it back into the saucepan, or simply push through a strainer, to give it a smooth consistency. Check the seasoning and reheat the sauce.

TO SERVE: this sauce can be served with any pasta, and is a good substitute for Fresh Tomato Sauce (see recipe above) when you are short of time.

MUSHROOM AND TOMATO SAUCE

SERVES 4

40 g/1½ oz butter
1 tablespoon olive oil
2 large onions, peeled and chopped
1×425 g/15 oz can Italian peeled
tomatoes
200 g/7 oz button mushrooms, chopped
2 cloves garlic, peeled and crushed
3 tablespoons tomato purée
120 ml/4 fl oz white wine
2 tablespoons chopped parsley
freshly ground black pepper

Melt the butter and the olive oil in a saucepan over a moderate heat and gently cook the onions until they are soft and transparent. Add the tomatoes with their liquid, mashing the whole tomatoes with a fork. Add the mushrooms, garlic, tomato purée, white wine and parsley, and season with pepper to taste. Simmer the sauce for 5 minutes.

TO SERVE: cook and drain 225 g/8 oz tagliatelle. Toss in a little butter, top with the sauce and serve immediately.

SEAFOOD SAUCE

SERVES 6

1 tablespoon olive oil
1 small carrot, peeled and chopped
1 stalk celery, chopped
1 onion, peeled and chopped
1 clove garlic, peeled and crushed
1 kg/2 lb uncooked prawns, peeled and
  cleaned
120 ml/4 fl oz brandy
1 kg/2 lb tomatoes, peeled and seeded
575 ml/19 fl oz dry white wine
freshly ground black pepper
salt
12 large mussels, scrubbed
1 tablespoon fresh chopped herbs, such as
  thyme, marjoram, parsley

Place the olive oil in a large saucepan over a moderate heat. Add the carrot, celery, onion and garlic. Fry lightly until the onion is transparent. Add the uncooked prawns. Shake the pan to toss the prawns about, add the brandy and flame. Take out 12 prawns and reserve them for a garnish. Add the tomatoes, 500 ml/18 fl oz white wine, pepper and salt. Cover the pan and cook until the mixture is slightly thickened. Purée the sauce in a blender, then strain it back into the pan, pounding the mixture with a wooden spoon to extract all the flavour. Discard the solids in the strainer.

Place the mussels in a saucepan with the remaining white wine and set over a fierce heat, shaking the pan frequently until they open (this only takes 3-4 minutes), discard any that do not open, and remove the meat.

Bring the sauce to the boil for a few minutes to reduce it slightly. Add the mussels, the reserved prawns and the fresh chopped herbs.

TO SERVE: any pasta is suitable for this sauce.

SPAGHETTI NERI

(Spaghetti with Squid Ink Sauce)

SERVES 4-6

3 medium cuttlefish (ink squid)
1 medium red onion, peeled
1 clove garlic, peeled
5 tablespoons olive oil
500 ml/18 fl oz dry white wine
1 small fresh tomato or 100 g/4 oz
  canned Italian tomatoes, drained
500 ml/18 fl oz chicken or beef stock
salt
freshly ground black pepper
sea salt, to cook pasta
450 g/1 lb dried spaghetti, preferably
  Italian
scant ½ teaspoon red pepper flakes

TO MAKE THE SAUCE: clean and cut the cuttlefish. Keep the ink glands.

Finely chop the onion and garlic together on a board. Heat the oil in a saucepan and, when it is hot, add the chopped ingredients and sauté until lightly golden brown (about 10 minutes). Add the squid and sauté for 3 minutes longer. Then add the wine and evaporate it very slowly (about 30 minutes).

Pass the tomato through a food mill. Heat the stock to boiling point.

Remove the saucepan containing the squid from the heat and place a strainer over the pan. Put the ink glands in the strainer and mash them with a spoon until most of the ink has been squeezed out. Pour 250 ml/8 fl oz of the stock through the mashed glands to extract the remaining ink.

Return the saucepan to the heat and add the strained tomatoes. Season to taste and simmer, uncovered, for about 20 minutes, adding the remaining hot stock as needed.

TO COOK THE PASTA: bring a large saucepan of water to the boil. Add sea salt to taste. Add the pasta and cook until *al dente*.

At this point the sauce should be reduced and the squid pieces completely tender. Sprinkle the red pepper flakes over the sauce, stir, and simmer for 1 minute longer.

TO SERVE: drain the pasta in a large colander and transfer it to a large serving dish. Pour the squid ink sauce over and toss the pasta well. Serve the dish hot.

SPAGHETTI CON VONGOLE

(Spaghetti with Clam Sauce)

Garlic is not essential to this recipe but it certainly adds flavour! It can be used whole and then discarded; otherwise it can be crushed, which gives a stronger flavour.

SERVES 4-6

120 ml/4 fl oz olive oil
½ teaspoon hot pepper flakes
2-3 cloves garlic, peeled (optional)
225 g/8 oz canned clams
450 g/1 lb spaghetti
salt
freshly ground black pepper
2 tablespoons freshly chopped parsley

In a large frying pan heat the oil with the pepper flakes and garlic. Remove the pan from the heat, add the clams with their can juices and return to the heat. Cook the spaghetti in boiling salted water, drain and add to the clams. Mix quickly, season to taste and pour into a hot serving dish.

TO SERVE: sprinkle with parsley and serve the pasta and sauce immediately.

Spaghetti Neri makes an audacious first course, full of deep-sea flavours.

TAGLIATELLE ALLA FRANTOIANA

(Rabbit and Black Olive Sauce with Tagliatelle)

SERVES 8

*3 small rabbits, weighing in all about
   2 kg/4 lb, livers reserved
25 g/1 oz unsalted butter
120 ml/4 fl oz olive oil
100 g/4 oz pancetta or prosciutto, diced
1 small red onion, peeled and chopped
3 medium carrots, peeled and chopped
2 medium stalks celery, chopped
leaves from 10 sprigs Italian parsley,
   chopped
1 clove garlic, peeled
250 ml/8 fl oz red wine
salt
freshly ground black pepper
4 tablespoons tomato purée
600 ml/1 pint beef stock
20 black Greek olives, stoned and
   chopped finely*

Wash the rabbit well. Cut it in pieces and cook in salted water for 5 minutes. This will remove the gamey flavour. Wash again and drain well.

Melt the butter and oil in a large frying pan and sauté the pancetta and rabbit, a few pieces at a time, until they are golden brown. Add the chopped vegetables, parsley and garlic and fry again for 3-4 minutes. Add the wine and cook to evaporate it. Season with salt and pepper. Dissolve the tomato purée in the beef stock and add half of this stock to the pan.

Cover the pan and simmer the rabbit for about 1 hour or until cooked, adding the remaining stock as needed.

Five minutes before the rabbit is cooked, remove the rabbit pieces to a serving dish, cover with foil and keep it warm. Add the black olives and chopped livers to the sauce, season to taste and keep it hot while you cook the pasta.

TO SERVE: serve with home-made tagliatelle, cooked very briefly and tossed with a little unsalted butter. Place the pasta on a serving dish, arrange the rabbit pieces on top and pour the sauce over. Garnish with whole black olives and chopped Italian parsley.

Summer is the time for tomato pasta with Ham, Cream and Mushroom Sauce.

HAM, CREAM AND MUSHROOM SAUCE

SERVES 4

25 g/1 oz butter
75-100 g/3-4 oz button mushrooms, sliced
4 slices cooked ham, chopped
1 clove garlic, peeled and crushed
freshly chopped basil, to taste
salt
freshly ground pepper
300 ml/½ pint single cream

Melt the butter in a saucepan over a moderate heat. Lightly sauté the mushrooms. Stir in the ham, garlic and basil and season to taste. Add the cream and heat through, stirring constantly without letting the sauce boil.

TO SERVE: fresh tomato noodles, cooked and lightly tossed in a little butter, would be the perfect type of pasta to serve with this sauce, adding delicate colour. Garnish with freshly grated Parmesan cheese and chopped parsley or basil.

CHICKEN LIVER SAUCE

SERVES 4

1 tablespoon olive oil
25 g/1 oz butter
1 medium onion, peeled and chopped finely
a few sprigs of fresh rosemary, chopped finely
100 g/4 oz chicken livers, cut in small pieces
200 g/7 oz lean veal, minced coarsely
500 ml/18 fl oz beef stock
2 tomatoes, peeled and chopped
salt
freshly ground black pepper

Heat the oil and butter together in a frying pan over a moderate heat. Add the chopped onion and rosemary. When the onion is softened and yellow, add the livers and veal and cook until slightly browned. Stir in the beef stock, a little at a time, using as much as is necessary to keep the sauce moist until the meat is cooked through. Add the tomatoes and cook until the sauce is thickened and the flavour well concentrated. Season with salt and pepper to taste.

TO SERVE: this full-flavoured sauce goes well with tagliatelle, topped with freshly grated Parmesan cheese.

RAGÙ ALLA BOLOGNESE

(Bolognese Sauce)

SERVES 6

225 g/8 oz lean steak, chopped finely
225 g/8 oz lean boneless pork, chopped finely
50 g/2 oz bacon or prosciutto, chopped
1 tablespoon olive oil
1 clove garlic, peeled
1 small onion, peeled and chopped finely
1 tablespoon chopped fresh parsley
1 bay leaf
1×425 g/15 oz can tomatoes
120 ml/4 fl oz white wine
120 ml/4 fl oz water
2 tablespoons tomato purée
salt
freshly ground black pepper
a little grated nutmeg
1 tablespoon chopped fresh basil
25 g/1 oz butter or 2 tablespoons single cream (optional)

In a mixing bowl combine the steak, pork and bacon or prosciutto, using a fork to make an evenly textured mixture. Heat the oil in a large saucepan over a moderate heat. Add the meat, garlic, onion, parsley and bay leaf and cook, stirring frequently to break up the meat until it is nicely browned and the onion and garlic soft and golden. Discard the garlic.

Add the tomatoes and the can juices, wine, water, tomato purée, salt, pepper and nutmeg. Reduce the heat, cover the pan and simmer for 1 hour. Add the basil and cook for 1 minute longer. Remove the saucepan from the heat and discard the bay leaf.

If you are using either butter or cream, stir it in just before serving.

TO SERVE: outside Italy Bolognese Sauce is most often served on top of spaghetti. In Italy, it would be well mixed with the spaghetti (or tagliatelle) before being presented at the table, with a knob of butter on top.

FETTUCCINE WITH FOUR CHEESES

SERVES 6

100 g/4 oz Swiss cheese, such as Emmenthal or Gruyère
100 g/4 oz fontina cheese
100 g/4 oz mozzarella cheese
350 ml/12 fl oz warmed milk
100 g/4 oz butter, melted
100 g/4 oz freshly grated Parmesan cheese
salt and freshly ground black pepper

Cut the Swiss cheese, fontina and mozzarella into small cubes. Place them in a saucepan with the warm milk and leave to stand until the cheeses become soft but do not melt completely.

TO SERVE: place 450 g/1 lb cooked fettuccine in a heated serving dish. Pour over the melted butter, half the Parmesan and the cheese sauce. Season with salt and pepper. Toss the pasta to mix the cheeses. Sprinkle with the remaining Parmesan.

CHAPTER TWO

RICE ACCOMPANIMENTS

Nutritious and versatile, rice deserves its place in history as an adaptable, attractive accompaniment on a variety of entertaining occasions

ARROZ VERDE

(Green Rice)

SERVES 4

250 g/9 oz long-grain rice
3 tablespoons peanut or safflower
   oil
120 ml/4 fl oz water
1 small bunch Italian parsley
3 sprigs fresh coriander
3 large cos lettuce leaves
2 canned green chillies
¼ small onion, peeled and chopped
   roughly
1 clove garlic, peeled and chopped
   roughly
750 ml/1¼ pints chicken stock
salt

Cover the rice with hot water and let it soak for about 20 minutes. Transfer it to a strainer, and rinse it well in cold water. Then leave to drain thoroughly – about 15 minutes.

In a heavy pan, heat the oil until it begins to smoke. Give the rice a good shake and stir it into the oil. Fry over a high heat, turning the rice thoroughly from time to time, until it is pale golden. Tip the pan to one side, holding the rice back with a wide metal spatula, and carefully drain off the oil.

Pour the cold water into a blender. Add the parsley, coriander, lettuce, chillies, onion and garlic, and blend until smooth, adding more water only if it becomes absolutely necessary to release the blades of the blender.

Add the blended ingredients to the rice and fry over a high heat, stirring constantly and scraping the bottom of the pan until the rice is almost dry. Add the stock and season lightly with salt. Cook over a medium heat for about 15 minutes until all the liquid has been absorbed and small air holes appear in the surface of the rice.

Cover the pan with a lid or foil and cook for 5 minutes longer. Turn off the heat and let the rice continue to cook in its own steam for 20-30 minutes.

SIMPLE FRIED RICE

SERVES 4

2-3 tablespoons olive oil
2 small shallots, peeled and chopped
   finely
1 green pepper, chopped
   finely
200 g/7 oz long-grain rice
1 litre/1¾ pints chicken stock
salt
freshly ground black pepper

Heat the oil in a frying pan. Add the shallots and green pepper and fry over a moderate heat until just tender. Add the rice, stirring it around the pan until it is transparent. Do not let it turn brown.

Meanwhile, pour the stock into a saucepan and bring it to the boil. Add the hot stock to the rice a tablespoon at a time, stirring continuously until the liquid is absorbed. Continue adding the stock in this way until it has all been absorbed and the rice is cooked (about 15-20 minutes). Season to taste, and serve immediately.

Simple but perfect, a creamy risotto depends on an assembly of the finest ingredients.

The distinctively fine flavour of Risotto al Brut makes it a perfect first course.

RISOTTO AL BRUT

(Risotto with Dry Vermouth)

SERVES 6-8

*4 tablespoons olive oil
1 medium onion, peeled and chopped
½ carrot, peeled and chopped
500 g/1¼ lb Arborio rice
1 litre/1¾ pints hot chicken stock
salt and freshly ground black pepper
50 g/2 oz butter
2 tablespoons bone marrow, melted
250 ml/8 fl oz dry white Italian vermouth,
  or more if necessary
225 g/8 oz freshly grated Parmesan cheese*

Heat the oil in a saucepan over a moderate heat. Fry the onion and carrot slowly until the onion is translucent. Add the rice and cook, stirring, until each grain of rice is coated with oil.

Cook the rice with the stock as for Risotto (see page 15). After 15 minutes of cooking, season to taste and stir in the butter, the melted marrow and the vermouth. Cook until the vermouth evaporates – about 2-3 minutes. Add half the grated Parmesan, stirring it in so that it melts completely. Check the seasoning, and add more vermouth if necessary.

TO SERVE: transfer the risotto to individual bowls and top each serving with the remaining Parmesan. Serve immediately.

RISOTTO TRICOLORE

(Three-coloured Risotto)

SERVES 4-6

*75 g/3 oz butter
1 large onion, peeled and chopped finely
500 g/1¼ lb Arborio rice
250 ml/8 fl oz dry white wine
2 litres/3½ pints chicken stock
3 tablespoons chopped Italian parsley
1 tablespoon chopped fresh basil
1 tablespoon tomato purée
150 g/5 oz freshly grated Parmesan cheese
salt*

Melt half the butter in a large saucepan. When the butter foams, add the onion and fry over a medium heat until it is pale yellow. Add the rice and mix well to coat the grains with butter. Add the wine and cook, stirring constantly, until the wine has evaporated. Stir in 120-250 ml/4-8 fl oz of stock and continue to cook, still stirring, until the liquid is absorbed. Continue cooking and stirring the rice, adding more stock a little at a time, until 250 ml/8 fl oz remains.

Divide the rice into 3 equal portions. Put 1 portion of rice into each of 2 small saucepans, leaving the third portion in the original pan. Add the parsley and basil to one pan and tomato purée to the second, leaving the third pan as it is. Continue cooking and stirring, incorporating the last of the stock, until the rice in each pan is tender but firm to the bite. Divide the remaining butter and half the Parmesan cheese equally between the pans and mix well to blend with the cooked rice. Season with salt.

TO SERVE: arrange the rice in a large, warm serving dish with white rice in the middle and red and green on each side. Serve immediately, with the remaining Parmesan cheese in a separate bowl.

Risotto Tricolore is a brilliantly colourful addition to any menu.

TURKISH PILAF

SERVES 8-10

400 g/14 oz long-grain rice
25 g/1 oz butter
1 small onion, peeled and chopped finely
salt and freshly ground black pepper
1 litre/1¾ pints boiling chicken stock
1 bay leaf
1×5 cm/2 inch piece cinnamon stick,
  broken into 2 or 3 pieces
75 g/3 oz raisins
75 g/3 oz dried apricots, diced

Rinse the rice in a strainer under cold running water until the water runs clear. Drain the rice thoroughly before cooking.

Melt the butter in a heavy saucepan over a low heat, add the onion and cook it gently until it is soft and golden. Stir in the rice, season with salt and pepper and cook the mixture, stirring frequently, until the rice becomes transparent.

Pour in the boiling stock, and add the bay leaf, cinnamon stick, raisins and dried apricots. Bring the mixture back to the boil, then lower the heat, cover the pan tightly and cook very gently for about 20 minutes or until all the liquid is absorbed and the rice is tender (small holes will appear in the surface). Remove the lid and cook, uncovered, for 1-2 minutes more. Fluff the rice up with a fork before serving.

PERSIAN RICE SALAD

SERVES 6-8

350 g/12 oz long-grain rice
2 slices fresh ginger, peeled and chopped
  finely
1 teaspoon ground cumin
1 teaspoon ground coriander
½ teaspoon ground nutmeg
6 shallots, peeled and chopped finely
2 teaspoons chopped chives
75 g/3 oz raisins, soaked in boiling water
  for 5 minutes and drained
75 g/3 oz sultanas, soaked in boiling
  water for 5 minutes and drained
1 tablespoon grated orange rind
75 g/3 oz toasted pine nuts
about 120 ml/4 fl oz olive oil
salt
freshly ground black pepper

Cook the rice according to Method 1 described on page 15. While still warm, transfer it to a mixing bowl and add the spices, shallots, chopped chives, raisins, sultanas, grated orange rind and pine nuts – reserving a few pine nuts for a garnish – quickly one by one, working them in with a fork to keep the texture light and open while blending the flavours evenly. Pour the oil all over the salad in a thin stream, still stirring, in order to moisten the rice without making it mushy. Season to taste.

Spoon the salad into a shallow serving dish and garnish with the reserved pine nuts. Serve the salad while still warm or at room temperature.

SRI LANKAN RICE

SERVES 6-8

750 g/1¾ lb long-grain rice
750 ml/1¼ pints water
1 tablespoon ghee

ACCOMPANIMENTS:
50 g/2 oz cashew nuts
150 g/5 oz sultanas, fried gently in butter
pappadums, broken into triangles
mango chutney
Malay pickle and lime pickle

Wash the rice thoroughly in several changes of water until the water runs clear. Place the rice, water and ghee in a large saucepan with a tightly fitting lid, or use a rice cooker. Set the pan over a moderate heat and bring to the boil. Reduce the heat and leave to simmer until all the liquid is absorbed and the rice is cooked and dry – 40 minutes.
TO SERVE: transfer the rice to a large warmed serving platter. Scatter the cashew nuts and sultanas over the top and arrange the pappadums fan-wise around the edge. Serve the chutney and pickles in separate bowls.

SAFFRON RICE

SERVES 6

50 g/2 oz butter
1 large onion, peeled and chopped finely
450 g/1 lb long-grain rice
900 ml/1½ pints hot chicken stock
a good pinch of saffron threads
2 teaspoons salt
freshly ground black pepper

Presented with care, Sri Lankan Rice is as attractive as it is delicious.

Heat the butter in a heavy saucepan over a moderate heat. Fry the onion until it is golden, but do not let it burn. Add the rice and fry for 2-3 minutes, stirring to coat the grains thoroughly with butter. Add the boiling stock and saffron. Bring back to the boil. Lower the heat, cover the pan and cook for 20 minutes. The rice is ready when it has absorbed all the liquid and is tender to the bite. Season to taste and transfer it to a warmed serving dish. Fluff it up with a fork and serve immediately.

SPICED BASMATI RICE

Even though this recipe is for Indian basmati rice, any long-grain, fine-quality rice can be used instead.

SERVES 6

1 teaspoon leaf saffron, loosely packed,
  roasted and crumbled
2 tablespoons warm milk
350 g/12 oz basmati or long-grain rice
1.5 litres/2½ pints water
1¼ teaspoons salt
2 tablespoons vegetable oil
5 cardamom pods
2 cinnamon sticks, approximately
  7.5 cm/3 inches long

In a small container, soak the saffron in the warm milk. Wash the rice well in plenty of cold water. Soak it in a bowl with 1 litre/1¾ pints of the water and ½ teaspoon salt for 30 minutes, then drain and reserve.
    Heat the oil over a medium heat in a 2-3 litre/3½-5½ pint heavy-bottomed saucepan (with a tight-fitting lid – to be used later), put in the cardamom pods and cinnamon sticks, and stir a few times. Add the rice, and cook, stirring constantly for about a minute.
    Add the remaining water and salt. Bring

to the boil, cover and reduce the heat to very low. Cook for 20 minutes. Lift off the cover. Gently but quickly mix the rice with a fork, turning it around a little. Pour the saffron milk in 2 or 3 streaks over the rice. Cover and keep cooking for another 10 minutes or until the rice is quite done.
TO SERVE: turn the rice on to a platter with a fork, in order to keep the grains whole.

MEAGADARRA

SERVES 4

225 g/8 oz green lentils
100 g/4 oz brown rice
1.25 litres/2¼ pints water
1 large onion, peeled and sliced finely
3 tablespoons olive oil
a little low-sodium salt
freshly ground black pepper

TO SERVE:
1 warm hard-boiled egg per serving or
  250 ml/8 fl oz plain yoghurt

Pick over the lentils and wash them in a colander. Wash the rice. Put both in a saucepan with the cold water and bring to the boil. Reduce the heat and cook, covered, for 30-35 minutes, until the lentils and rice are tender and the water has been absorbed. Set aside and keep warm.
    Fry the sliced onion in the olive oil until it is well browned. Turn the lentils and rice into a bowl. Fork them through lightly, seasoning with a little salt and pepper. Scatter the fried onions on top. Leave to cool for about 45 minutes before serving.
TO SERVE: top with warm hard-boiled eggs or serve with a bowl of plain yoghurt.

INDONESIAN RICE

SERVES 8

1 chicken stock cube
¼ teaspoon salt
4 cardamom pods
1 stick cinnamon
1 teaspoon turmeric powder
225 g/8 oz long-grain rice
150 g/5 oz butter
50 g/2 oz cashew nuts

GARNISH:
10 fresh dates, cut in strips
zest of 2 limes, blanched in boiling water
* and refreshed*

Bring a large saucepan of water to the boil
with the stock cube, salt and spices. Then
add the rice, stir once, and cook, uncovered, for 12-15 minutes, until the rice is
tender.

While the rice is cooking, melt 25 g/1 oz
butter in a small heavy saucepan over a
moderate heat. Cook the cashews in the
butter until nicely browned all over. Do not
let them burn.

Strain the cooked rice well. Mix in the
remaining butter with a fork.

TO SERVE: spoon the rice into a large dish.
Garnish with the cashew nuts, dates and
lime zest cut in strips. Serve immediately.

Indonesian Rice is a perfect savoury
partner for a feast of simply barbecued
meats with aubergines, salad and exotic
sauces and relishes.

WILD RICE WITH SHIITAKE AND ONIONS

SERVES 6

12 large dried shiitake (Oriental black
    mushrooms)
1 tablespoon peanut oil
about 750 ml/1¼ pints chicken stock or
    canned chicken broth
275 g/10 oz wild rice, rinsed well and
    drained
315 g/10 oz small white onions
25 g/1 oz unsalted butter
salt
freshly ground black pepper

In a bowl combine the mushrooms, the oil and 250 ml/8 fl oz of the stock, warmed; let the mixture stand for 30 minutes, and strain the liquid into a bowl through a fine sieve lined with a coffee filter or a double thickness of rinsed and squeezed cheesecloth. Cut off the mushroom stems, reserving for use in soups or stocks. Quarter the caps.

Add enough of the remaining stock to the mushroom liquid to measure 600 ml/1 pint and in a large saucepan combine the liquid with the wild rice. Bring to a rolling boil over a high heat, stirring constantly, then reduce the heat and cook the wild rice, covered, at a bare simmer, stirring occasionally, for 40-45 minutes or until it is just tender. (Begin testing the rice after 30 minutes, adding more stock if necessary.) Stir in the mushrooms and simmer the mixture, covered, for 10 minutes.

To a saucepan of boiling water add the onions, return the water to the boil, and drain the onions in a colander. Refresh the onions under cold water, peel them, and return them to the saucepan. Add 120 ml/4 fl oz of the remaining stock and simmer the onions, covered, for 10 minutes, or until they are just tender. Add half the butter and

toss the onions over a moderately high heat until they are glazed and the liquid is reduced to a syrup. Combine the onions with the rice mixture and the remaining butter. Add salt and pepper, stirring gently. Transfer to a warmed platter to serve.

STEAMED VEGETABLE RICE WITH COURGETTES AND CARROTS

SERVES 4

450 g/1 lb rice
225 g/8 oz courgettes
225 g/8 oz young carrots
1½ teaspoons salt
2 tablespoons melted butter

Wash the rice and boil it in its own volume of water for 8 minutes. Remove from the heat. Clean and cut the courgettes and carrots into 2.5 cm/1 inch lengths. Parboil them for 1½ minutes, drain and place in 4 large serving bowls. Sprinkle with salt and melted butter while still hot. Put the partly cooked rice on top of the vegetables in the bowls. Place the bowls in a steamer and steam for 12 minutes. Serve immediately.

WILD RICE PILAF

SERVES 8-10

225 g/8 oz wild rice
50 g/2 oz butter
1 onion, peeled and chopped finely
225 g/8 oz long-grain rice
½ teaspoon turmeric
1 teaspoon allspice
1 teaspoon cinnamon
600 ml/1 pint chicken stock
100 g/4 oz toasted pine nuts
salt and freshly ground black pepper

Place the wild rice in a saucepan, cover with water and soak for 1 hour. Place the pan over a moderate heat and bring the rice to the boil. Reduce the heat and simmer for 20 minutes. Drain and set aside.

Melt the butter in a large frying pan set over a moderate heat and cook the onion until soft. Add the wild rice, long-grain rice and spices and cook, stirring, until the long-grain rice turns semi-transparent and yellow. Reduce the heat, add the stock, cover and cook gently for about 20 minutes until the rice is tender and has absorbed all the stock. Stir in the pine nuts and season to taste. Transfer to a serving dish and serve immediately.

RICE AS A SIDE DISH

Rice as an accompaniment can be used either as part of a menu which is entirely Indian, Japanese, Italian or whatever is suitable, or as a surprise element in other recipes. In the former case, try to be authentic in every detail. In India, for example, rice is often cooked without salt when served with highly flavoured curries that have a liquid consistency. The slight sweetness of Sri Lankan Rice (page 31) goes well with mild-to-medium strength chicken or lamb curries and Saffron Rice makes a good partner for hot dry meat curries as well as fish and shellfish. Italian classics, such as ossobuco or saltimbocca are offset well by the beautiful Risotto Tricolore (page 29), with a little less Parmesan cheese (also good with a simple roast or fish dish).

CHAPTER THREE

FIRST COURSES

Blend innovation and imagination with tradition, using rice and pasta as the basis for a collection of entertaining and appetizing first courses

PASTA SALAD WITH AUBERGINE AND BASIL

SERVES 8

2 medium aubergines
salt
250 ml/8 fl oz olive oil
2 large onions, peeled and sliced
4 ripe tomatoes, peeled, seeded, chopped
2 sweet red peppers, sliced
275 g/10 oz button mushrooms
torn basil leaves, to taste
375 g/13 oz mixed white and green
  fettuccine
salt and freshly ground black pepper
²/₃×375 g/13 oz jar pomodori secchi
  (Italian dried tomatoes in oil, available
  from delicatessens)
1×440 g/14 oz can artichoke hearts,
  drained and cut in half

GARNISH:
shredded basil leaves

Cut the aubergines into 2.5 cm/1 inch cubes and sprinkle with salt. Leave to stand for 2 hours to sweat. Pat dry with a paper towel. Heat the oil in a large saucepan and fry the onions gently until they are soft and golden but not browned. Add the chopped tomatoes and cook until the mixture thickens. Add the cubed aubergine, and continue to cook until the mixture is soft. Add the sweet red peppers, mushrooms and basil and cook for a further 5 minutes.

Cook the pasta in a large saucepan of boiling salted water until it is *al dente*. Drain and quickly refresh it under cold running water. Drain again well. Place in a large serving bowl with the aubergine mixture and toss well together. Slice the dried tomatoes and arrange them on top of the salad with the artichoke halves. Sprinkle over two thirds of the oil from the tomato jar and garnish with shredded basil leaves. Add salt and freshly ground pepper to taste.

PASTA WITH SPINACH AND BEETROOT LEAVES

SERVES 8

450 g/1 lb tender young spinach leaves
leaves from 2 bunches young beetroot
4 tablespoons olive oil
2 cloves garlic, peeled and crushed
250 ml/8 fl oz single cream (optional)
1 kg/2 lb fettuccine or tagliatelle
salt
freshly ground black pepper
100 g/4 oz freshly grated Parmesan cheese

Wash the vegetable leaves very well in cold water, dry thoroughly and slice them into narrow strips. Heat the oil in a large frying pan over a moderate heat and add the crushed garlic. Add the leaves and stir-fry until tender. Add the cream if using.

Cook the pasta in a large saucepan of boiling water until it is *al dente*. Drain well and add to the frying pan. Toss the leaves and the pasta together. Season to taste and transfer to a warmed serving dish. Sprinkle the Parmesan on top and serve.

Anticipation of culinary delights is one of the keenest pleasures to be had from the best meals.

INDIVIDUAL MUSHROOM RAVIOLI

SERVES 6

PASTA:
450 g/1 lb plain flour
4 eggs
6 egg yolks
pinch of salt
3 tablespoons olive oil
1 egg, beaten, to seal

FILLING:
100 g/4 oz butter
1.5 kg/3 lb very fresh button mushrooms,
* sliced finely*
2 tablespoons water
salt and freshly ground black pepper

SAUCE:
24 large field mushrooms, sliced
25 g/1 oz butter
salt
freshly ground black pepper
juices from the mushroom filling
120 ml/4 fl oz single cream

TO MAKE THE PASTA: use a food processor as described on page 10. Cut the dough into 4 pieces for ease of handling and put it through the roller until you reach the second-finest thickness. Alternatively, roll out and stretch the dough manually until it is as fine as a piece of cloth. Allow the rolled-out strips to stand and dry until they begin to curl at the edges.

TO MAKE THE FILLING: melt the butter in a large saucepan. Add the sliced button mushrooms and cook over a moderate heat for 2-3 minutes, tossing the mushrooms to coat them in butter. Add the water, season to taste and cook for a few minutes more, until the mushrooms are just tender. Lift them out of the pan, reserving all the juices, and set aside to keep warm.

TO MAKE THE SAUCE: place the sliced field mushrooms in a saucepan with the butter, season to taste and toss them over a moderate heat for 2-3 minutes. Add the reserved juices and the cream and cook, stirring gently and without letting the cream boil, for 5 minutes. Keep hot.

TO ASSEMBLE AND SERVE: cut out 24 large circles of pasta with a fluted 13 cm/5 inch round pastry cutter. Brush the edges of 12 circles with beaten egg and pile an equal amount of mushroom filling in the centre of each circle. Place the remaining circles of pasta on top. Press well together to seal.

Cook the ravioli in boiling salted water for 9 minutes. Lift out with a slotted spoon and place on individual heated plates. Pour on the hot sauce and serve at once.

BABY SPINACH RAVIOLI

SERVES 8

Pasta all'Uovo (see page 10) made with
* 350 g/12 oz flour*
6 large spinach leaves
2-3 sprigs fresh parsley
salt and freshly ground black pepper

Prepare the pasta and roll it out to 2 large sheets. Remove and discard the stalks from the spinach leaves. Wash the leaves thoroughly in cold water. Bring a saucepan of water to the boil and dip each leaf in the boiling water. Refresh the leaves in cold water, strain and pat dry. Place them in a blender or food processor with the parsley and blend briefly, or chop them roughly on a board. Season to taste.

Spread out one sheet of pasta dough. Place teaspoons of the spinach mixture about 4 cm/1½ inches apart on the dough. Cover with the second sheet. With a 4 cm/1½ inch round pastry cutter, separate the ravioli. Pinch the edges together firmly.

Carefully place the ravioli in a pan of boiling salted water. They are cooked when they rise to the surface – about 4 minutes.

TO SERVE: serve in hot broth, a light sauce, or with butter and Parmesan cheese.

INSALATA DI TORTELLINI

(Tortellini Salad)

SERVES 4-6

FILLING:
4 tablespoons olive oil
40 g/1½ oz butter
200 g/7 oz young veal, trimmed and cut
* in cubes*
75 g/3 oz prosciutto, diced
75 g/3 oz mortadella, cubed
6 fresh sage leaves, chopped coarsely
2 eggs
freshly grated nutmeg
100 g/4 oz freshly grated Parmesan cheese
freshly ground black pepper

PASTA:
450 g/1 lb Italian durum wheat pasta
* flour (if unavailable, use a strong bread*
* flour or continental flour)*
5 eggs, beaten
2 tablespoons olive oil
2 teaspoons salt
2 tablespoons water
1 beaten egg, to seal

TO SERVE:
3-4 tablespoons olive oil
1-2 tablespoons white wine vinegar
salt
freshly ground black pepper
2 tablespoons mixed fresh herbs such as
* chives, chervil, basil and flat-leaved*
* parsley, chopped very finely*

TO MAKE THE FILLING: heat the oil and butter in a frying pan over moderate heat and fry the veal, prosciutto, mortadella and sage until the veal is cooked. Chill and process in a food processor with the eggs, nutmeg and Parmesan cheese. Season with pepper.

TO MAKE THE PASTA: sift the flour into a mixing bowl. Make a well in the middle and add the eggs, oil, salt and water. Draw the flour into the centre with a wooden spoon, stirring until the mixture forms a dough. Turn

it out on to a floured marble slab and knead until the dough becomes elastic. This dough will take quite a lot of kneading. Although it will be rather crumbly at first, continue kneading - do not add any extra liquid. Roll the dough out to a 3 mm/⅛ inch thin sheet. Using a pastry cutter, cut out circles of pasta about 4 cm/1½ inches in diameter.

TO MAKE THE TORTELLINI: place a little of the filling in the centre of each circle of pasta.

Brush the edges very lightly with beaten egg. Fold each circle into a half-moon shape, then twist it around your index finger and pinch the ends together to make the classic tortellini shape.

Cook the tortellini in a large saucepan of boiling salted water for about 1 minute only. Drain them well, transfer to a large serving bowl, and leave to cool.

TO SERVE: drizzle the olive oil over the pasta, and sprinkle with vinegar. Season with salt and pepper to taste and sprinkle over the herbs. Toss the salad gently once or twice before serving.

PASTA CON LA RICOTTA

(Pasta with Ricotta Cheese)

SERVES 4-6

250 g/9 oz tagliatelle
175 g/6 oz ricotta cheese
50 g/2 oz freshly grated Parmesan
  cheese
pinch of grated nutmeg
salt
freshly ground black pepper
15 g/½ oz butter

Heat the oven to 160°C/325°F/Gas Mark 3.

Cook the pasta in a large saucepan of boiling salted water until it is *al dente*. Drain well and transfer to an ovenproof serving dish.

Beat the ricotta cheese in a mixing bowl until it is smooth. Add the Parmesan. Season with nutmeg, salt and pepper. Stir the cheese mixture into the pasta with the butter and place the dish in the oven for 2 minutes so that the cheese begins to melt. Serve immediately.

Serve Pasta con la Ricotta when the cheese is just on the point of melting.

GREEN AND WHITE NOODLES WITH MUSHROOMS AND PARSLEY

SERVES 8

1 kg/2 lb very fresh button mushrooms
100 g/4 oz butter
salt
freshly ground black pepper
1 clove garlic, peeled
450 g/1 lb fresh plain tagliatelle
450 g/1 lb fresh green tagliatelle
1 tablespoon olive oil
2 tablespoons freshly chopped parsley

Trim the mushrooms and clean them with a paper towel. Melt the butter in a large frying pan over a moderate heat and add the mushrooms. Season well and squeeze in garlic through a press according to taste. Toss the mushrooms until they are almost cooked. Turn off the heat and cover the pan.

Cook the plain and green tagliatelle together in a large saucepan of boiling salted water until it is *al dente*. Drain well, pour in the oil, season with salt and pepper and toss with 2 forks.

Reheat the mushrooms gently and stir in the parsley.

TO SERVE: spoon the pasta into individual serving bowls and arrange the mushrooms in the centre.

SPAGHETTI WITH COURGETTES

SERVES 4

6 courgettes, about 10 cm/4 inches long
salt
350 g/12 oz spaghetti
4 tablespoons olive oil
freshly ground black pepper
50 g/2 oz freshly grated Parmesan
  cheese

Cut the unpeeled courgettes into thin slices, sprinkle them with a little salt and leave to stand in a colander for about 20 minutes to drain. Pat dry with paper towels.

Cook the pasta in a large saucepan of boiling salted water until it is *al dente*. Drain, toss it in 2 tablespoons of olive oil and add black pepper to taste.

Heat the remaining olive oil in a frying pan over a high heat and fry the courgette slices very quickly until they are brown on the outside, but still crisp to the bite.

Toss the courgettes with the spaghetti. Transfer to a warmed serving bowl, sprinkle with the grated Parmesan and serve immediately.

CHOOSING A FIRST COURSE

First impressions are important, and the first course of a meal needs particular consideration. If you decide to start with a simple, satisfying dish which precedes a complex but light main course, watch the quantities carefully, so that guests' appetites are not dulled. Such dishes benefit from the use of interesting garnishes or lively accompanying wine and should be served on attractive and appropriate china. A dish that is pleasing to the eye is a great stimulant to the palate. A glance at the range of pasta available gives a hint of how well pasta can solve the first course problem. Appetising and colourful garnishes can be created by clever cooks using green or purple-tinged salad leaves, scarlet radishes and peppers, yellow baby corn cobs and coloured shellfish.

TAGLIATELLE WITH ROASTED PINE NUTS

SERVES 4

225 g/8 oz prosciutto or coppa
1 teaspoon olive oil
225 g/8 oz roasted pine nuts
350 g/12 oz fresh tagliatelle
salt
12 slices bone marrow, cut in
  3 mm/1/8 inch round slices
2 tablespoons freshly chopped
  parsley

Cut the prosciutto or coppa into thin strips. Place the olive oil in a frying pan over a moderate heat and cook the prosciutto briskly until crisp, taking care not to burn the oil. Quickly stir in the pine nuts and remove the pan from the heat.

Cook the pasta in a large saucepan of boiling salted water until it is *al dente*. When it is ready, drain and transfer it to warmed individual dishes. Divide the prosciutto and pine nut mixture equally between the dishes and combine it with the cooked pasta.

Garnish each serving with 3 slices of bone marrow, sprinkle chopped parsley on top and serve immediately.

Essentially informal and quickly prepared as many pasta dishes are, they can be extremely stylish. Tagliatelle with Roasted Pine Nuts proves the point.

ORANGE FETTUCCINE WITH SCALLOPS

SERVES 4

250 ml/8 fl oz fish stock
3 strips orange zest
pinch of mixed Provençal herbs (bay,
*   thyme, rosemary and basil)*
sea salt and freshly ground white pepper
450 g/1 lb scallops, cleaned
50 g/2 oz unsalted butter
½ leek, washed and cut in fine julienne
1 medium young carrot, peeled and cut
*   in fine julienne*
1 stalk celery, cut in fine julienne
1 tablespoon olive oil
500 g/1¼ lb orange-flavoured fettuccine
2 egg yolks
4 tablespoons single cream

Place the fish stock in a medium saucepan with 1 strip orange zest, the herbs, salt and pepper. Bring to the boil, reduce the heat and add the scallops. Poach them in the simmering liquid for 2-3 minutes, depending on their size. Do not overcook the scallops or they will toughen. Lift them out with a slotted spoon and keep warm.

Strain the poaching liquid and discard the solids. Reduce the liquid by half. Remove from the heat but keep warm.

Cut the remaining 2 strips of orange zest into fine julienne and blanch in boiling water for 3 minutes. Drain and refresh.

Melt the butter in a heavy-bottomed pan over a moderate heat. Add the blanched orange zest and the vegetables. Cook gently to soften while retaining their colours.

Bring a large saucepan of salted water to the boil. Add the olive oil and cook the fettuccine until *al dente*. While the pasta is cooking, place the poaching liquid over a moderate heat and whisk in the egg yolks and cream to thicken it. Do not allow it to boil. Season to taste. Fold the scallops into the sauce.

Drain the fettuccine and arrange on 4 heated plates. Spoon the sauce and scallops over the pasta. Sprinkle the prepared vegetables on top and serve immediately.

SHELL PASTA WITH PRAWNS AND MANGE TOUT

SERVES 4

225 g/8 oz pasta shells (2 sizes)
75 g/3 oz mange tout
225 g/8 oz prawns, cooked
75 g/3 oz fresh bean sprouts
40 g/1½ oz butter
1 tablespoon oil
1 sprig fresh rosemary, chopped
freshly ground black pepper

Cook the pasta in boiling salted water until it is *al dente* (about 8-10 minutes).

Prepare the mange tout by removing the tops and strings. Shell the prawns. Wash the bean sprouts under cold running water to remove as many of the husks as possible. When the pasta is almost cooked add the mange tout to the boiling water and cook for 1 minute. Drain well and place in a bowl.

Melt the butter with the oil in a pan over a moderate heat. Add the prawns and toss until they are just heated through. Add them to the pasta with the melted butter and oil from the pan. Stir in the bean sprouts, tossing them well with two forks. Sprinkle with the rosemary and black pepper, and serve.

Left *Orange Fettuccine with Scallops;*
Opposite *Shell Pasta with Prawns and Mange Tout.*

RED PEPPER PASTA WITH LOBSTER AND BASIL

SERVES 8

PASTA:
3 whole sweet red peppers
175 g/6 oz plain flour
6 egg yolks
2 tablespoons olive oil

SAUCE:
750 g/1½ lb cooked lobster
½ bottle Chardonnay/white wine
6 shallots, chopped finely
5 sprigs parsley
5 sprigs fresh thyme
1 bay leaf
3 black peppercorns
500 ml/18 fl oz single cream

GARNISH:
40 g/1½ oz basil leaves, cut into fine strips

TO MAKE THE PASTA: place the peppers under a hot grill until they are charred and cooked. Remove the skins and seeds. Chop the flesh roughly and purée in a blender. Combine the purée with the flour and make the pasta dough (see page 10 for method). Put the dough through the pasta machine on the 'angel hair' setting.

TO MAKE THE LOBSTER SAUCE: remove the flesh from the lobster shells and cut into medallions. Reserve the shells. Place the wine, shallots, parsley, thyme, bay leaf, peppercorns and lobster shells in a saucepan. Add enough cold water to cover. Bring to the boil, then lower the heat and simmer for 20 minutes. Strain the liquid into a clean pan and discard the solids. Bring to the boil, and let the liquid reduce to 120 ml/4 fl oz. Add the cream and continue to cook until the sauce has reduced to a thick consistency. Keep the sauce warm.

TO COOK THE PASTA: cook the pasta in a large pan of boiling salted water to which the oil has been added, until it is *al dente*. (As it is so fine it will cook very quickly.) When it is cooked, drain the pasta and combine it well with the sauce, turning them together with two forks.

TO SERVE: transfer the pasta and sauce to a warmed dish and garnish with the lobster medallions and finely sliced basil leaves.

LOBSTER RAVIOLI WITH TRUFFLES

SERVES 8

PASTA:
450 g/1 lb plain flour
4 eggs
good pinch of salt

FILLING:
2 small lobster tails, cooked
1 white truffle, chopped (reserve liquid from jar – see below)
pinch of salt
freshly ground black pepper

SAUCE:
5 tablespoons Madeira
200 ml/⅓ pint hot chicken stock
250 ml/8 fl oz crème fraîche
½ tablespoon reserved truffle juice

GARNISH:
1 white truffle, chopped

TO MAKE THE PASTA: see page 10 for method. Roll the dough into 2 thin sheets or put it through the finest roller of the pasta machine.

TO PREPARE THE FILLING: remove the flesh from the lobster shells and chop it roughly. Place it in a bowl with the truffle, salt and pepper and mix well.

TO PREPARE THE RAVIOLI: lay 1 sheet of pasta on a large floured board and place 24 table-spoonsful of the lobster mixture at even intervals all over the pasta. Cover with the second sheet of pasta and separate the ravioli with a large cutter. Pinch the edges together firmly to seal them.

TO MAKE THE SAUCE: place the Madeira in a small saucepan. Bring to the boil and let it reduce by half. Add the chicken stock, reduce again, and add the crème fraîche. Boil until the sauce thickens and add the reserved truffle juice. Keep the sauce warm while you cook the ravioli.

TO COOK AND SERVE THE RAVIOLI: bring a large saucepan of salted water to the boil. Carefully place the ravioli in the pan and boil for 4 minutes (no longer, or the lobster will toughen). Lift them out with a slotted spoon as soon as they are ready.

Divide the ravioli between 8 individual dishes. Pour over the sauce and garnish with chopped truffle.

PRESENTING PASTA

Ribbon and long pastas and all pasta served with sauces are best presented in deep dishes with a rim like old-fashioned soup plates. Place the dish on a service plate so that the fork and spoon can be rested tidily. Look out for modern pasta settings in a variety of designs, some with a suitably Italian theme.

Lobster Ravioli with Truffles – the most elegant of dinner party openers.

FIRST COURSES WITH RICE

BROWN RICE WITH FRESH HERB SAUCE

SERVES 4

225 g/8 oz brown rice

SAUCE:
250 ml/8 fl oz coconut milk
generous quantities (at least
 4 tablespoons each) of chives, fresh
 green coriander, mint, basil,
 tarragon and dill
6 spring onions
250 ml/8 fl oz plain yoghurt
250 ml/8 fl oz soured cream (or double
 the amount of yoghurt)

Cook the rice according to Method 3 on page 15.

TO MAKE THE SAUCE: make the coconut milk following the instructions given under Nasi lemak on page 86 but using 75 g/3 oz coconut and 250 ml/8 fl oz boiling water. Wash the herbs and chop them roughly, setting some aside for a garnish. Chop the spring onions finely. Place in a blender or food processor with the yoghurt, coconut milk and cream and purée until the mixture is a creamy, green colour.

Pour the mixture into a small, heavy saucepan or double boiler and heat through gently without boiling.

TO SERVE: when the rice is cooked, transfer it to a serving dish and sprinkle the reserved herbs on top. Serve the warm sauce separately in a bowl or jug.

SUSHI

These rolls can be made several hours in advance and kept covered in the refrigerator. Serve at room temperature.

SERVES 8

475 g/1 lb 2 oz short-grain rice
600 ml/1 pint water
grated rind of 1 lemon
2 teaspoons finely chopped pickled
 ginger
2 teaspoons finely chopped chives
sheets of dried seaweed

DRESSING:
4 tablespoons rice vinegar
3 tablespoons caster sugar
2 teaspoons soy sauce
2 tablespoons dry sherry

TO SERVE:
wasabi (Japanese horseradish)
soy sauce

TO PREPARE THE RICE: rinse the rice several times in cold water and drain it well. Place it with the water in a large saucepan over a high heat. When it comes to the boil, cover the pan, reduce the heat to low and cook for 15 minutes. Remove the pan from the heat, keep it covered and let it stand for 10 minutes.

Place all the dressing ingredients in a screwtop jar and shake it well to blend them thoroughly.

Transfer the rice to a large shallow dish and toss it gently together with the lemon rind, pickled ginger and chives. Mix in the dressing with a fork. Cool the rice quickly by fanning it.

TO ASSEMBLE THE SUSHI: spread the rice mixture on the sheets of dried seaweed and roll them up. Cut them in 2.5 cm/1 inch lengths with a sharp knife. Arrange the little rolls on a flat tray or dish with the rice side up (see picture right).

TO SERVE: sprinkle a little wasabi on top of each roll. Serve with a dish of soy sauce to dip the rolls.

VERSATILE RICE

Although it has a long association with Asian countries, rice which is now grown around the world takes on a variety of international flavours. A boon to the busy cook, its versatility and simple cooking methods mean it is an ideal solution for first courses. The secret of successful starters is that they should be satisfying yet not so filling as to spoil the enjoyment of what lies ahead. In this respect rice – like pasta – has grown in popularity as the basis of such small but appetizing courses. Naturally rice gains from attractive presentation – and this is where much can be learned from the Japanese, whose reverence for food, especially rice, stems from their need to maximize limited resources. Small amounts of very fresh ingredients are an essential part of their cookery. *Gohan*, the Japanese word for meal, also means rice. Italian-based rice dishes, too, make full use of local resources such as tomatoes and mushrooms, cheeses and herbs.

Excellent as a first course, Sushi also make exquisite canapés suitable for any special occasion.

RISOTTO CON PORCINI

(Rice with Dried Mushrooms)

SERVES 6

35 g/1¼ oz dried porcini or cèpes
350 ml/12 fl oz warm water
1.2 litres/2 pints chicken stock or brown
  stock or canned broth
2 tablespoons olive oil
25 g/1 oz chopped onion
50 g/2 oz unsalted butter
400 g/14 oz Arborio rice
100 g/4 oz freshly grated Parmesan cheese
salt
freshly ground pepper

In a bowl let the mushrooms soak in the water combined with 250 ml/8 fl oz of the stock, warmed, and 1 tablespoon of the oil for 30 minutes, or until they are softened. Strain the liquid into a saucepan through a sieve lined with a coffee filter or a double thickness of rinsed and squeezed cheese-cloth, and rinse the mushrooms.

Heat the mushroom liquid with the remaining stock over a moderately low heat until the mixture is hot and keep it warm.

In a heavy saucepan cook the onion in half the butter and the remaining table-spoon of oil over a moderate heat, stirring, until it is softened. Add the rice and cook, stirring, for 3-5 minutes, or until the rice is partially translucent. Add 120 ml/4 fl oz of the hot stock mixture and cook the rice over a low heat, stirring, until the liquid is almost absorbed. Add all but 2 tablespoons of the

Risotto con Funghi, a rustic dish, is well suited to satisfy keen autumn appetites, and is served locally in the Veneto with tumblers of hearty red wine.

remaining stock mixture, 120 ml/4 fl oz at a time, stirring and cooking the mixture until the liquid is absorbed after each addition and adding the mushrooms after the risotto has been cooking for 20 minutes. The mixture should be creamy but the rice should be *al dente*.

Remove the pan from the heat and stir in the remaining butter, the 2 tablespoons of reserved stock mixture, one-third of the Parmesan, and salt and pepper to taste.

Serve the risotto with the remaining Parmesan.

RISOTTO CON FUNGHI

(Rice with Fresh Mushrooms)

SERVES 6

1 kg/2 lb fresh mushrooms
1 tablespoon olive oil
25 g/1 oz chopped parsley
1 clove garlic, peeled and chopped finely
freshly ground white pepper
400 g/14 oz Arborio rice
1 litre/1¾ pints boiling vegetable stock
  (more if necessary)
salt
100 g/4 oz butter
100 g/4 oz freshly grated Parmesan cheese

Wash and chop the mushrooms. Heat the oil in a large saucepan and cook the mush-rooms over a moderate heat with the parsley, garlic and pepper for 5 minutes, stirring occasionally. Stir in the rice and cook for 1 minute. Add the stock a little at a time as the rice absorbs the liquid, stirring constantly. Add salt to taste.

When the rice is *al dente*, add the butter and Parmesan. Mix well and transfer to a heated serving dish. Leave to rest for a few minutes before serving.

WILD RICE SALAD WITH WALNUT DRESSING

SERVES 4

200 g/7 oz wild rice
100 g/4 oz mange tout, topped and tailed
⅔×375 g/13 oz jar pomodori secchi
  (Italian dried tomatoes), drained
2 medium carrots, peeled and cut into
  fine julienne
75 g/3 oz walnuts, chopped

DRESSING:
120 ml/4 fl oz cup walnut oil
2 tablespoons white wine vinegar
1 tablespoon Dijon mustard
salt
freshly ground black pepper

Cook the rice as described for Breasts of Quail on Wild Rice (see page 51), using 1 litre/1¾ pints water.

Blanch and refresh the mange tout. Pat them dry on paper towels. Cut the tomatoes into slivers.

Transfer the cooked rice to a bowl and combine it with the peas, tomatoes, carrots and nuts, using 2 forks to keep the texture light.

TO MAKE THE DRESSING: place all the ingre-dients in a screwtop jar and shake well to amalgamate or mix in a blender for 30 seconds.

TO SERVE: mix the dressing into the salad, blending it in evenly with a fork. Leave to cool for 30 minutes or more before serving.

WATERZOOI DE POISSON

(Flemish Fish Soup)

SERVES 4-6

225 g/8 oz long-grain rice
50 g/2 oz butter
3 stalks celery, chopped
1 kg/2 lb mixed white fish fillets
salt
freshly ground black pepper
175 ml/6 fl oz dry white wine
¼ teaspoon dried thyme
1 bay leaf
1 sprig fresh basil

Cook the rice according to Method 1 on page 15. Set aside and keep warm while making the soup.

Melt half the butter in a deep, heavy saucepan, over a moderate heat. Add the celery and arrange the fish fillets on top. Season well with salt and pepper. Add the wine and just enough cold water to cover the fish. Add the herbs and the remaining butter, cut in small pieces. Bring the liquid just to the boil. Immediately reduce the heat, cover the pan and simmer very gently until the fish is cooked, about 10-15 minutes, depending on the thickness of the fillets.

Lift the cooked fish out of the soup with a slotted spoon. Remove and discard the skin and flake the flesh into large pieces with a fork.

TO SERVE: divide the hot rice between 4 or 6 soup bowls. Arrange the fish on top. Remove the bay leaf and sprig of basil from the cooking liquid and pour it carefully over the fish; alternatively serve it separately in other bowls.

PORK AND CRAB PORCUPINE BALLS

SERVES 4-6

400 g/14 oz short-grain rice
6 dried Chinese mushrooms
3 shallots
100 g/4 oz water chestnuts
225 g/8 oz minced pork
1×170 g/5½ oz can crab
½ teaspoon crushed garlic
½ teaspoon grated ginger
small sprig of coriander
1 egg
225 g/8 oz cooked long-grain rice,
    prepared as described on page 15 and
    drained thoroughly

Soak the short-grain rice in cold water for 1 hour. Drain and spread it out to dry on a tea towel. Soak the mushrooms for 30 minutes in warm water. Trim the shallots and cut them into thin slices, including the green tops. Using the steel blade of a food processor, chop the water chestnuts for 2-3 seconds. Add the mushrooms, shallots, pork, crab, garlic, ginger, coriander and egg and process until well mixed. Alternatively, chop the water chestnuts finely and combine them in a large mixing bowl with the other ingredients, blending well to obtain a smooth consistency.

Form the mixture into small balls, 2-3 cm/ about 1 inch in diameter, and coat with the dried rice. Steam in a Chinese steamer for 20 minutes.

Serve hot with fiery Chilli Sauce (see recipe right).

CHILLI SAUCE

50 g/2 oz chilli powder
750 g/1½ lb sugar
750 ml/1¼ pints white vinegar
350 g/12 oz sultanas
1 tablespoon crushed garlic
1½ teaspoons ginger
3 tablespoons salt
soy or tomato sauce (optional)

Combine all the ingredients in a stainless steel saucepan. Bring to the boil, reduce the heat and simmer until the sultanas are tender. Process half the mixture at a time in a food processor, using the steel blade. Alternatively, press through a sieve.

Store in sterilized bottles (empty vinegar bottles are ideal).

RISI E BISI

(Rice and Peas)

SERVES 6

1 kg/2 lb unshelled peas
1 litre/1¾ pints water
salt
50 g/2 oz unsalted butter
2 tablespoons olive oil
100 g/4 oz pancetta or prosciutto, diced
1 medium stalk celery, chopped
leaves from 10 sprigs Italian parsley,
    chopped
120 ml/4 fl oz dry white wine

RISOTTO:
750 ml/1¼ pints beef stock
400 g/14 oz Arborio rice
40 g/1½ oz unsalted butter
3 heaped tablespoons freshly grated
    Parmesan cheese
salt and freshly ground black pepper

Pork and Crab Porcupine Balls are quite fragile and best served in the steamer.

Shell the peas and set them aside. Put the pea pods in a saucepan with the water and a small pinch of salt. Bring to the boil and cook until the liquid is reduced to 250 ml/8 fl oz. Strain the liquid into a bowl and discard the pods.

Melt the butter and oil in a large frying pan and fry the pancetta or prosciutto until it is lightly browned. Add the celery and parsley leaves and fry a little longer. Add the peas and white wine and cook for 10-15 minutes until the peas have absorbed the wine.

TO MAKE THE RISOTTO: add the reserved liquid to the beef stock in a large saucepan and bring to the boil. Add the rice to the pea mixture in the frying pan and toss for about 5 minutes to fry the rice. Add a soup ladle of boiling stock to the frying pan and, as it cooks and is absorbed into the rice, add more simmering stock, ladle by ladle. It will take 15-20 minutes to cook the rice. The risotto should be creamy but not too liquid.

Remove the pan from the heat and stir in the butter and Parmesan cheese. The cheese will thicken the risotto. Season to taste and serve at once.

ACCOMPANYING DRINKS

With certain foods, especially those of Asian origin, wine is not appropriate yet refreshing drinks are needed with highly seasoned food. Serve green tea, cold beer and mineral water, as well as jugs of iced juice and iced water. *Saké* (rice wine) is served warm and kept in an insulated container throughout the meal.

BREASTS OF QUAIL ON WILD RICE

SERVES 4

150 g/5 oz wild rice
750 ml/1¼ pints water
oil for deep frying
1-2 potatoes, peeled and cut into
  julienne
75 g/3 oz butter
12 quail breasts, skinned

SAUCE:
3 teaspoons red wine vinegar
250 ml/8 fl oz red wine
250 ml/8 fl oz stock (from quail bones)

GARNISH:
4 hard-boiled quail eggs, peeled
cooked beetroot slices
chopped chives
sprigs of thyme
sage flowers

TO PREPARE THE WILD RICE: wash under cold, running water. Place the water in a saucepan and bring it to the boil. Add the rice and boil steadily for 5 minutes. Remove from the heat, cover the pan and let it stand for 1 hour. Drain and rinse the rice. Cook in a large pan of boiling salted water until tender – about 35-40 minutes.

TO MAKE THE POTATO BASKETS: heat the oil for frying in a large saucepan. Dry the potato strips on paper towels. Using 2 small strainers, arrange the strips in a criss-cross fashion in one strainer and gently press the other into it to make a basket shape. Still holding the strainers together, carefully immerse them in the hot oil until the potato is golden. Drain on paper towels. Repeat this process with the remaining potato

Breasts of Quail on Wild Rice are presented in a nest of julienne potatoes.

strips to make 3 more baskets.

TO COOK THE QUAIL: melt the butter in a large frying pan, add the quail breasts and cook over a low to moderate heat for about 2 minutes on each side or until cooked.

TO MAKE THE SAUCE: place the vinegar and red wine in a heavy-bottomed pan and simmer until thickened and reduced by half. Add the stock and reduce again. Keep warm.

TO SERVE: place a quarter of the wild rice in the centre of each plate. Over this, fan 3 quail breasts, making room in the centre for a potato basket. Place a quail egg in each basket and decorate with a piece of beetroot cut out with a heart-shaped cutter. At the last moment, spoon the sauce over the breasts and add a few chopped chives, a sprig of thyme and a sage flower for a garnish (see picture left).

STUFFED TOMATOES WITH LEMON SAUCE

SERVES 6

10-12 medium tomatoes
2 tablespoons olive oil
1 medium onion, peeled and chopped
  finely
1 clove garlic, peeled and crushed
3 tablespoons finely chopped parsley
450 g/1 lb chopped lamb or beef
1 teaspoon salt
3 tablespoons long-grain rice
1 teaspoon dried oregano
4 tablespoons white wine
50 g/2 oz pine nuts
500 ml/18 fl oz beef stock

LEMON SAUCE:
175 ml/6 fl oz reserved beef stock
2 eggs
2 tablespoons lemon juice

Cut the tops off the tomatoes and scoop out the pulp. Chop it finely and set it aside. Heat the oil in a large saucepan over a moderate heat and fry the onion until golden. Add the garlic, parsley, tomato, meat, salt, rice, oregano and wine. Cover and simmer for 20 minutes, stirring occasionally. Mix in the pine nuts, and simmer until the juices evaporate. Spoon the mixture into the hollowed tomatoes and place them in a large frying pan. Pour in the stock, cover and simmer for 3-4 minutes until the tomatoes are tender. Lift out the tomatoes and place them on a serving dish. Keep them warm. Reserve the stock to make the sauce.

TO MAKE THE LEMON SAUCE: measure the reserved stock. Boil it down to 175 ml/6 fl oz. Beat the eggs in a bowl and blend in the lemon juice. Pour in the hot stock, stirring constantly. Return the sauce to the pan and set it over a low heat, stirring occasionally until thickened. Spoon the sauce around the tomatoes and serve.

RICE FILLINGS FOR VEGETABLES

Vegetables stuffed with rice make attractive, appetising first courses. Try tomatoes as well as sweet red, green or yellow peppers, aubergine, artichokes or large baked onions. Suggestions for fillings based on long-grain rice include:

- prawns or shrimps, diced tomato, basil
- flaked smoked fish, chopped egg, chopped chives
- walnuts, garlic and sultanas
- anchovies, pimiento, black olives
- mushrooms, diced ham, pineapple

CHAPTER FOUR

LIGHT LUNCHES

Just right for lunches – or light suppers – each recipe has flair,
and highlights the delicious versatility of rice and pasta for entertaining

LIGHT PASTA DISHES

FETTUCCINE ALFREDO

This is the simplest way to present fettuccine but it is also the most difficult because it has to be perfect and the ingredients have to be the best.

SERVES 6

450 g/1 lb home-made fettuccine
1 tablespoon olive oil
salt

SAUCE:
175 g/6 oz butter, softened
100 g/4 oz freshly grated Parmesan cheese
freshly ground pepper

Cut up the butter in small chunks and spread it on a hot serving platter.

Set a large saucepan of water over a high heat. When the water boils, take out 2-3 tablespoons and pour it over the butter; pour the olive oil into the pan. Add the salt and the fettuccine. Stir and in 1 minute when the fettuccine surfaces – don't bother to taste – remove the pan from the heat. Drain quickly to leave the fettuccine moist.
TO SERVE: pour the fettuccine on to the platter over the butter. Start tossing and add the Parmesan, a little at a time, mixing deftly the fettuccine, butter and Parmesan, and lastly, add a few twists of black pepper. Serve immediately, perhaps with a crisp salad.

BOW TIE PASTA PRIMAVERA

SERVES 6

1×450 g/1 lb packet bow tie pasta
2 medium carrots, peeled and cut in batons
1 bunch asparagus, cut in 4 cm/1½ inch lengths
1 large head of broccoli, broken into tiny florets
4 medium tomatoes, seeded and cut in strips
100 g/4 oz mange tout, topped and tailed
185 g/6 oz butter
1 clove garlic, peeled and crushed lightly
salt and freshly ground black pepper

Bring a large saucepan of salted water to the boil and cook the pasta according to the instructions on the packet.

While it is cooking, prepare the vegetables. Have ready a saucepan of boiling salted water. Drop in the carrots and cook them for about 4 minutes. Lift them out with a strainer or slotted spoon and set aside in a large bowl to keep warm. Repeat the process with the asparagus and broccoli, placing them in the bowl with the carrots. The vegetables should be tender but not overcooked, and should retain their fresh colour. Cook the tomatoes and mange tout in the same way but for 1 minute only to heat them through, and place them in the bowl with the other vegetables.

Melt the butter in a small saucepan with the garlic clove over a gentle heat. Remove the garlic and pour the flavoured butter over the vegetables. When the pasta is cooked, drain it well and add it to the vegetables, tossing well to combine all the ingredients. Season to taste and serve at once.
TO SERVE: this lovely light pasta dish really needs no accompaniment. Follow with fromage frais and fresh strawberries or cherries or any other soft fruit.

Fresh flowers and crisp linen set the scene for an informal lunch – simple but extremely elegant.

TOMATO PASTA SALAD

SERVES 8

SAUCE:
¼×375 g/13 oz jar pomodori secchi
  (Italian dried tomatoes) with ¼ oil
250 ml/8 fl oz olive oil
4 tablespoons wine vinegar
1 small onion, peeled and chopped finely
1 teaspoon anchovy paste
salt and freshly ground black pepper
pinch of sugar

SALAD:
450 g/1 lb fresh tomato-flavoured
  fettuccine (see page 10)
1 sweet red pepper, cut in julienne
225 g/8 oz young carrots, peeled and cut
  in julienne
1 bunch chives, chopped
½× 130 ml/4½ fl oz jar capers, drained

GARNISH:
baby tomatoes

TO MAKE THE SAUCE: place all the ingredients in a blender or food processor and blend until smooth. Alternatively, chop the tomatoes and place them in a mixing bowl with the oil and vinegar. Mix together well and add the onion and anchovy paste. Stir together thoroughly and season with salt, pepper and sugar.
TO MAKE THE SALAD: cook the fettuccine in a large saucepan of boiling salted water until *al dente*. Drain the cooked pasta well, refresh it under cold water, and drain again. Mix it with the sauce immediately, turning it well so that it is evenly coated. Add the prepared sweet red pepper, carrots, chives and capers and toss well. Season to taste.
TO SERVE: serve cool, garnished with baby tomatoes. Accompany by crusty French bread and salade frisée.

NUTMEG NOODLES WITH MORELS AND CREAM

SERVES 4

PASTA:
3 large eggs
2 tablespoons water
225 g/8 oz plain flour
1 teaspoon salt
1 teaspoon freshly grated nutmeg

MUSHROOM SAUCE:
25 g/1 oz dried morels
300 ml/½ pint double cream
¼ teaspoon salt

TO MAKE THE PASTA: beat the eggs with the water in a bowl. In a food processor combine well the flour, ¾ teaspoon of the salt, and the nutmeg and, with the motor running, add enough of the egg mixture in a stream to form a ball of dough. Knead the pasta dough on a floured surface for 3-5 minutes, or until it is springy to the touch, and let it stand, covered with a teatowel, for 30 minutes.
TO MAKE THE SAUCE: place the mushrooms in a small bowl and add enough warm water to just cover them. Leave to soak for 2 minutes, or until they are just soft enough to cut. Strain the liquid into a bowl through a fine sieve lined with a coffee filter or a double thickness of rinsed and squeezed cheesecloth. Reserve it for use in soups or stews. Trim the bases of the mushrooms, halve the mushrooms lengthwise, and rinse them well to remove all traces of soil and grit.
  In a small saucepan combine the mushrooms, the cream, and the remaining ¼ teaspoon salt. Set the pan over a low heat and bring the cream to a bare simmer. Remove from the heat and let the mixture stand, covered, for 1 hour.
TO ASSEMBLE AND COOK: knead and roll the pasta dough and cut it into fettuccine. Using a slotted spoon, transfer the mushrooms to a plate. Simmer the cream, stirring all the time, until it is reduced to about 150 ml/¼ pint, and return the mushrooms to the pan.
  Bring a large saucepan of salted water to the boil and cook the fettuccine for 2-5 minutes, or until they are *al dente*. Drain the fettuccine and transfer them to a heated bowl. Toss with the mushroom sauce and serve immediately.
TO SERVE: accompany with asparagus tips.

PASTA WITH CREAMY HERB SAUCE

SERVES 6

450 g/1 lb fresh green angel hair pasta or
  vermicelli

SAUCE:
350 ml/12 fl oz single cream
50 g/2 oz clarified butter
½ teaspoon salt
pinch of grated nutmeg
pinch of cayenne pepper
25 g/1 oz freshly grated Parmesan cheese
25 g/1 oz finely chopped mixed fresh herbs
  (basil, thyme, watercress, Italian parsley,
  marjoram and chives)

TO MAKE THE SAUCE: place the cream, butter, salt, nutmeg and cayenne in a heavy-bottomed saucepan and simmer over a low heat for 15 minutes, stirring occasionally. Do not let the sauce boil. Whisk in the cheese and herbs and simmer while you cook the pasta in plenty of boiling salted water until *al dente*.
  When the pasta is cooked, drain it and divide it between 4 individual bowls. Top with the sauce and serve immediately.
TO SERVE: accompany this dish with a simple tomato salad.

FRITTATA DI SPAGHETTI

(Spaghetti Omelette)

A frittata is an open omelette in which any variety of cooked vegetables may be mixed into the eggs. After the omelette cake has been finished under the grill, it is cut into wedges. This is an unusual variation.

SERVES 4

SAUCE:
2 tablespoons olive oil
1 onion, peeled and chopped finely
500 g/1 lb tomatoes, peeled, seeded and
*   cut in small pieces*
1 clove garlic, peeled and crushed
salt
freshly ground black pepper
1 tablespoon chopped basil

OMELETTE:
350 g/12 oz spaghetti
50 g/2 oz butter
50 g/2 oz freshly grated Parmesan cheese
2 eggs
1 tablespoon chopped parsley
salt and freshly ground black pepper
2 tablespoons olive oil

Pasta with Creamy Herb Sauce makes the most of seasonal fresh herbs.

TO MAKE THE SAUCE: heat the oil in a frying pan set over a moderate heat. Fry the onion gently until it is translucent. Add the tomatoes, increase the heat and sauté, stirring to blend the tomatoes and onion, for 3-4 minutes. Add the garlic and season to taste. The tomatoes should be just cooked and the juice well reduced. Add the basil and set aside until you are ready to serve.

TO MAKE THE OMELETTE: bring a large saucepan of salted water to the boil and cook the spaghetti until *al dente*. Drain well and toss in butter. Stir in half the cheese carefully, so that the cheese melts and the strands of spaghetti do not stick together.

Beat the eggs in a bowl, just enough to mix the yolks and whites. Add the remaining cheese with the parsley, salt and pepper. Combine this mixture with the spaghetti.

Heat the oil in a large, heavy-bottomed frying pan over a gentle heat. Add the spaghetti mixture and spread it out evenly. Cook slowly for about 10-15 minutes, moving the pan so that the frittata does not stick.

While the frittata is cooking, reheat the sauce and heat the grill to high. When the frittata is just cooked, place it, still in the pan, under the grill briefly, to brown the top. Cut the frittata into wedges and transfer to 4 hot plates. Pour over the sauce and serve immediately.

TO SERVE: a good accompaniment would be courgettes and aubergines cut into matchstick strips, sautéed in good olive oil.

55

Using homemade pasta, Rotolo di Spinaci is stuffed with spinach and cheeses.

ROTOLO DI SPINACI

(Spinach and Pasta Roll)

SERVES 6-8

STUFFING:
1 kg/2 lb fresh spinach, washed and
  chopped finely
25 g/1 oz butter
1 shallot, peeled and sliced finely
400 g/14 oz ricotta cheese
1 egg
salt
freshly ground black pepper
grated nutmeg
50 g/2 oz freshly grated Parmesan cheese

PASTA:
3 large eggs
300 g/11 oz plain flour
1 tablespoon salt
extra flour to roll pasta

TO FINISH THE ROTOLO:
150 g/5 oz butter
7-8 fresh sage leaves, chopped
50 g/2 oz freshly grated Parmesan cheese

TO MAKE THE STUFFING: steam the spinach for about 3 minutes. Squeeze out the moisture.

Melt the butter in a small frying pan and fry the shallot until it is transparent. In a large bowl mix together the ricotta, egg, salt, pepper, nutmeg and Parmesan cheese. Combine the spinach and shallot with this mixture and blend well.

TO MAKE THE PASTA: see page 10. Roll it out to a square, thin sheet.

TO MAKE THE ROTOLO: spread the spinach and ricotta stuffing thickly and evenly on the sheet of pasta, leaving a border of about 4 cm/1½ inches all round. Roll the pasta into a sausage. Seal both ends by pressing down the pasta and folding the ends slightly.

Place the roll in a large piece of muslin, fold over the roll and tie at both ends with string. Half-fill a fish steamer with boiling salted water and lower the rotolo into it. Add more boiling water if necessary to cover. Cook for about 15 minutes. Lift out the cooked rotolo, remove the muslin and cut the rotolo into 2 cm/¾ inch slices.

TO FINISH THE ROTOLO: butter an ovenproof dish and arrange the slices on the butter. Heat the grill to high. Melt the remaining butter in a small saucepan and add the sage leaves. Sprinkle the slices of rotolo with Parmesan cheese. Pour the butter and sage mixture over the slices. Grill the dish until golden brown. Serve immediately.

TO SERVE: the rotolo can be served with tomato sauce (see page 21) and green salad.

GOAT CHEESE PASTA

SERVES 8

PASTA:
6 egg yolks
175 g/6 oz plain flour

SAUCE:
500 ml/18 fl oz single cream
100 g/4 oz goat cheese
salt and freshly ground black pepper

GARNISH:
30 pencil-thin asparagus spears
450 g/1 lb prepared scallops, prawns or shrimps
1 tablespoon caviar
2 tablespoons finely chopped chives

Make the pasta in a food processor according to the method described on page 10. Put the dough through a pasta machine on the 'angel hair' setting.

To make the sauce, place the cream and cheese in a small heavy-bottomed saucepan over a moderate heat. Cook, stirring, until the cheese has melted and the sauce is thick and smooth. Season to taste. Keep warm.

Blanch the asparagus. Cut the spears to even 10 cm/4 inch lengths, including tips.

Cook the pasta in boiling salted water until it is *al dente*. Heat the grill to moderate and cook the seafood. Do not overcook or cook too quickly or it will be tough.

Drain the cooked pasta and add it to the sauce, tossing well to coat the strands. Transfer to a serving dish and garnish with asparagus, seafood, caviar and chives.

TO SERVE: serve with crusty rolls and a refreshing cucumber salad.

SPINACH FETTUCCINE WITH SMOKED SALMON

SERVES 4

200 g/7 oz spinach fettuccine
salt
350 ml/12 fl oz single cream
1 tablespoon lemon juice
1 tablespoon freshly chopped mixed herbs – dill, basil, rosemary
100 g/4 oz smoked salmon, sliced and cut into strips

Cook the pasta in a large saucepan of boiling salted water until it is *al dente*.

While the pasta is cooking heat the cream through gently. Add the lemon juice and herbs. Let the cream reduce a little.

Drain the cooked pasta well and add it to the cream. Toss to incorporate the pasta thoroughly with the sauce. Add the smoked salmon strips, toss once more and transfer to a serving dish. Serve immediately.

TO SERVE: accompany with a watercress salad dressed with lemony vinaigrette and garnished with slices of hard-boiled egg.

SALAD OF NOODLES WITH CRAYFISH AND SMOKED SALMON

SERVES 6-8

250 g/8 oz smoked salmon, sliced thinly
1 teaspoon olive oil
500 g/1¼ lb fresh noodles
16 crayfish or Mediterranean prawns, cooked and peeled
1 teaspoon freshly chopped basil
1 teaspoon freshly chopped tarragon
24 ripe cherry tomatoes

VINAIGRETTE:
200 ml/⅓ pint walnut oil
4½ tablespoons white wine vinegar or tarragon vinegar
salt and freshly ground black pepper

GARNISH:
6 teaspoons salmon roe (optional)
fresh basil leaves

Prepare the vinaigrette dressing first. Mix all the ingredients together thoroughly either by processing briefly in a blender or placing them in a screwtop jar and shaking it vigorously. Cut the smoked salmon into 1 cm/½ inch squares.

Bring a large saucepan of salted water to the boil. Add the olive oil and throw the noodles into the boiling water. Cook for 1 minute. Drain the noodles, plunge them in iced water and drain thoroughly. Transfer the noodles to a large serving bowl.

Combine the crayfish, smoked salmon and chopped herbs with the noodles. Add the vinaigrette and toss all the ingredients in the dressing until they are well coated. Gently mix in the cherry tomatoes, reserving a few. Serve garnished with salmon roe, basil and the reserved cherry tomatoes.

TO SERVE: provide plenty of crusty French bread to mop up the juices.

WATERCRESS PASTA WITH MUSSELS IN WINE

SERVES 10-12

WATERCRESS PASTA:
75 g/3 oz watercress leaves
4 large eggs
4 egg yolks
1 teaspoon salt
750 g/1½ lb plain flour

MUSSELS:
5 dozen fresh mussels
2 cloves garlic, cut in half
500 ml/18 fl oz dry white wine

TO COOK AND DRESS THE PASTA:
175 ml/6 fl oz olive oil
50 g/2 oz soft butter
120 ml/4 fl oz fresh lemon juice
reserved juice from steamed mussels
6 medium tomatoes, peeled, seeded and
*   chopped in 1 cm/½ inch pieces*

Watercress Pasta with Mussels in Wine is a perfect dish for a light lunch.

TO MAKE THE PASTA: place the watercress, eggs, yolks and salt in a food processor and process with an on/off action for 2 minutes, or until the mixture is puréed and pale green. Sprinkle the flour evenly over the egg mixture and process again with an on/off action until small beads form. If the dough is too moist, add more flour a tablespoon at a time until beads form. Remove the mixture from the food processor and place it in a plastic bag. Set aside for 15 minutes.

Divide the mixture into 4 before rolling it out either by hand or with a pasta machine. Cut the pasta into fettuccine and let it dry slightly before using it.

TO COOK THE MUSSELS: wash the mussels in plenty of cold water. Remove and discard the beards. Throw away any mussels with broken shells or shells that have opened.

Place the cleaned mussels in a large bowl, cover with cold water and leave to stand for 3-4 hours, changing the water several times to clear the mussels of sand.

Drain the mussels and place them in a large covered saucepan with the garlic and wine. Cover the pan and steam the mussels over a low heat, shaking the pan gently, for 4-5 minutes until the shells open. Discard any unopened shells. Reserve as much as possible of the cooking juice. Remove most of the mussels from their shells, leaving 2-3 per serving in their shells to garnish the finished dish. Discard the empty shells and the pieces of garlic.

TO COOK AND DRESS THE PASTA: bring a large pan of salted water to the boil, add 2 tablespoons oil, drop in the pasta and cook for 10 minutes or until *al dente*. Drain well and return the pasta to the pot. Dress the pasta with the butter, the remaining olive oil, lemon juice and reserved cooking juice. Add half the shelled mussels and half the chopped tomatoes and toss well.

TO SERVE: place the pasta and mussel mixture and sauce in a large bowl, or divide for individual servings. Garnish with the remaining mussels, tomato pieces and reserved mussels in their shells. Provide French bread to mop up the dressing, and a salad of fresh watercress with quarters of lemon to squeeze over.

SPINACH TORTELLINI WITH CHILLI SAUCE

SERVES 4

½ tablespoon olive oil
450 g/1 lb spinach tortellini

SAUCE:
100 g/4 oz piece Italian salami, peeled
    and chopped
2 cloves garlic, peeled
1 teaspoon Dijon mustard
1-2 small dried chillies
15 g/½ oz Italian parsley leaves
100 g/4 oz pomodori secchi (Italian dried
    tomatoes in oil), drained
1-2 tablespoons lemon juice
pinch of dried oregano leaves
75-120 ml/3-4 fl oz virgin olive oil
1-1½ tablespoons freshly grated Parmesan
    cheese
salt and freshly ground black pepper

GARNISH:
basil leaves

TO MAKE THE SAUCE: in a food processor, blend the salami, garlic, mustard, chillies, parsley and tomatoes until the tomatoes are finely chopped. Add the lemon juice and oregano and slowly drizzle in the olive oil with the machine running. (Alternatively, chop the salami, garlic, chillies, parsley and tomatoes very finely and pound them together in a mortar. Place the mixture in a bowl and add the mustard, lemon juice and oregano. Stir well. Continue to stir as you slowly pour in the oil until an even consistency is obtained.)

Stir the Parmesan cheese into the sauce. Taste and adjust the seasoning if necessary. Cover, and refrigerate until ready to serve. The sauce can be made 1 day ahead.

TO COOK THE PASTA: bring a large saucepan of salted water to the boil, add the olive oil and tortellini and cook until *al dente*. Drain well and transfer to a warmed mixing bowl. Toss the pasta with a quarter of the sauce.

TO SERVE: spoon into individual warmed dishes. Top each serving with the remaining sauce and dress each with 2-3 fresh basil leaves. Serve immediately, with a simple green salad.

LASAGNE

The meat sauce may be made ahead, frozen and reheated.

BUFFET PARTY DISH FOR 20

salt
2 tablespoons vegetable oil
2 kg/4 lb lasagne

MEAT SAUCE:
4 tablespoons olive oil
4 onions, peeled and chopped finely
4 cloves garlic, peeled and crushed
2 kg/4 lb lean beef, minced
450 g/1 lb chicken livers, chopped finely
4×800 g/1 lb 12 oz cans tomatoes
250 ml/8 fl oz tomato purée
15 g/7½ oz freshly chopped basil
1 teaspoon dried oregano
250 ml/8 fl oz chicken stock
25 g/1 oz freshly chopped parsley
2-3 stalks celery, chopped
1 tablespoon plus 2 teaspoons salt
4 teaspoons sugar
freshly ground black pepper
3 bay leaves

FILLING:
50 g/2 oz butter
2 kg/4 lb ricotta cheese
2 kg/4 lb mozzarella cheese, sliced thinly
450 g/1 lb freshly grated Parmesan cheese

TO MAKE THE MEAT SAUCE: heat the oil in a large, heavy-bottomed saucepan over a moderate heat. Fry the onions and garlic for 5 minutes. Add the minced beef and the chopped livers and fry, stirring from time to time, until they are browned all over. Add all the remaining ingredients, combining them well, and reduce the heat. Simmer for about 1 hour.

TO COOK THE LASAGNE: bring a large saucepan of salted water to the boil. (It may be easier to divide the lasagne into smaller quantities and cook it in several batches.) Add a little oil to the water and throw in the pasta. Boil for 15 minutes or until *al dente*. Drain well and pour on a little oil to prevent the sheets sticking together.

TO ASSEMBLE: heat the oven to 180°C/350°F/ Gas Mark 4. Cover the bases of two 38×23 cm/15×9 inch well-buttered ovenproof dishes with some of the meat sauce. Cover with a layer of lasagne. Mix the ricotta cheese with 500 ml/18 fl oz of meat sauce. Spoon some of this mixture over the lasagne. Cover with a layer of mozzarella cheese and sprinkle with Parmesan. Continue the layers in this way until you have used all the ingredients, ending with a sprinkling of grated Parmesan cheese.

TO COOK AND SERVE: place the dishes in the oven and bake for about 1 hour, until the lasagne is bubbling and the cheese has thoroughly melted. When the lasagne is cooked, turn down the heat to 110°C/225°F/ Gas Mark ¼, and it will keep without spoiling for 30 minutes. Serve with crusty bread and a fresh green salad.

TIMBALE OF MACARONI WITH CHICKEN

SERVES 12

TIMBALE DOUGH:
5 egg yolks
50 g/2 oz caster sugar
225 g/8 oz butter, softened
450 g/1 lb plain flour
grated rind of 1 lemon
pinch of salt

BÉCHAMEL SAUCE:
40 g /1½ oz butter
50 g/2 oz plain flour
1 litre/1¾ pints milk
freshly grated nutmeg
salt

FILLING:
1×1.5 kg/3-4 lb chicken, boned and cut
into small pieces
50 g/2 oz plain flour
salt
freshly ground black pepper
1 tablespoon olive oil
1 tablespoon butter
1 onion, peeled and chopped
1 tablespoon freshly chopped rosemary,
sage and thyme
175 g/6 oz shelled green peas
150 g/5 oz button mushrooms, sliced
250 ml/8 fl oz dry white wine
6 canned plum tomatoes, drained and
chopped
250 ml/8 fl oz hot chicken stock
2 tablespoons freshly grated Parmesan
cheese
450 g/1 lb fresh or dried macaroni
1 egg, beaten

TO MAKE THE TIMBALE DOUGH: place the egg yolks in a mixing bowl with the sugar and butter, and beat until pale and creamy. Sift in the flour, add the lemon rind and salt and rub in lightly with your fingertips. (Alternatively place all the ingredients in a food processor and blend until thoroughly mixed.) Form the dough into a ball, wrap it in a plastic bag, and leave to rest for 1 hour.

TO MAKE THE BÉCHAMEL SAUCE: melt the butter in a saucepan over a moderate heat. Stir in the flour and mix well to form a roux. Let it cook for 1 minute, still stirring. In another saucepan, bring the milk to the boil. Pour the milk slowly over the roux, whisking the mixture all the time. Reduce the heat and continue whisking until the sauce boils. Season to taste with nutmeg and salt, reduce the heat and simmer for 10 minutes.

TO MAKE THE FILLING: dust the chicken pieces with flour and sprinkle them with salt and pepper. Heat the oil in a large pan over a moderate heat and fry the chicken pieces until lightly golden all over. Remove them from the pan and set aside.

Melt the butter in the pan and cook the onion and herbs over a low heat until the onion is transparent but not browned. Return the chicken pieces to the pan and add the peas, mushrooms and wine. Increase the heat to bring the wine to the boil. Reduce the heat and simmer until it has completely evaporated. Add the chopped tomatoes and chicken stock, and continue to cook for about 20 minutes, until the liquid is well reduced. Stir in the Parmesan cheese and set aside.

Cook the macaroni in boiling salted water until it is *al dente*. Drain well. Combine the macaroni with the béchamel sauce. Add this mixture to the chicken and blend well.

Heat the oven to 220°C/425°F/Gas Mark 7.

TO ASSEMBLE THE TIMBALE: roll out the dough on a floured board. Use three-quarters of the dough to line a well-buttered 30 cm/ 12 inch spring-form pan, reserving the remaining dough to make a lid. Spoon the hot filling into the pan. Roll out the remaining pastry and place it on top of the timbale. Trim the edges, leaving enough to pinch the base and lid together firmly. Use the pastry trimmings to shape leaves to decorate the top of the timbale. Paint with beaten egg to glaze.

TO COOK AND SERVE: place the timbale on the centre shelf of the oven and bake for 35-40 minutes. Remove from the oven, and place on a flat serving dish or board. Loosen the spring-form and leave to stand for 20 minutes. Remove the spring-form and serve the timbale in slices, like a cake. Accompany with a crisp salad.

TOMATO FETTUCCINE WITH LAMB'S LIVER

SERVES 8

2 small lamb's livers
flour for dredging
salt
freshly ground black pepper
50 g/2 oz butter
4 rashers bacon, cut in strips
1 medium aubergine, sliced thinly
2 onions, peeled and cut in rings
1 small sweet red pepper,
peeled with a vegetable peeler and
cut in strips
1 small green pepper, peeled
with a vegetable peeler and cut
in strips
450 g/1 lb dried tomato fettuccine
2 tablespoons shredded basil leaves

Remove the skin from the livers and cut them into 1 cm/½ inch strips. Dust the strips with seasoned flour.

Melt half the butter in a frying pan set over a moderate heat and fry the bacon strips until cooked. Lift from the pan and

Freshly picked basil leaves provide a finish to Tomato Fettuccine with Lamb's Liver.

FETTUCCINE WITH PROSCIUTTO AND ASPARAGUS

SERVES 4

350 g/12 oz home-made fettuccine
25 g/1 oz butter
3-4 tablespoons hot water or chicken
stock
65 g/2½ oz shelled peas
225 g/8 oz asparagus, trimmed and cut
into 5 cm/2 inch bias lengths
2-3 cloves garlic, peeled and chopped
finely
100 g/4 oz prosciutto, cut into
julienne
120 ml/4 fl oz single cream
25 g/1 oz freshly grated Parmesan cheese
salt
freshly ground black pepper

Prepare the fettuccine according to the basic recipe on page 10, and cut into strips slightly narrower than 1 cm/½ inch.

Melt the butter in a medium saucepan over a moderate heat and add the water or chicken stock. Add the peas and asparagus and simmer for a few minutes, until the liquid is nearly evaporated. Add the garlic and prosciutto and continue to cook for a few more minutes. Cover the pan and set aside to keep warm.

Cook the fettuccine in a large saucepan of boiling salted water until it is *al dente*. Drain well.

Add the cream to the vegetables and prosciutto, then stir in the pasta. Toss the ingredients together over a gentle heat for a moment to coat the pasta with cream. Add half of the cheese and toss again. Season with salt and pepper and serve immediately, topped with the remaining cheese.

TO SERVE: serve with hot crusty bread and a salad of sliced tomatoes with a scattering of stoned black olives.

drain on paper towels. Fry the aubergine slices until brown and cooked. Drain on paper towels. Repeat this process with the onions and red and green peppers. Set the bacon and vegetables aside to keep warm.

Cook the fettuccine in a large saucepan of boiling salted water for 10-12 minutes, until *al dente*. Drain and keep hot while you cook the liver.

Melt the remaining butter in a large fry-ing pan and fry the liver strips until brown and only just cooked. Add the bacon and vegetables to the pan and toss them to-gether to heat through. Season to taste and toss in the shredded basil leaves.

TO SERVE: transfer the fettuccine to a warmed serving dish and spoon the liver mixture on top. This dish really needs no accompaniment.

GNOCCHI WITH PROSCIUTTO AND BROAD BEANS

SERVES 6

GNOCCHI:
750 g/1½ lb potatoes
150 g/5 oz plain flour

SAUCE:
350 ml/12 fl oz single cream
375 g/13 oz broad beans, shelled
12 sage leaves, chopped
225 g/8 oz prosciutto, chopped
salt
freshly ground pepper

TO SERVE:
freshly grated Parmesan cheese

TO MAKE THE GNOCCHI: cook the unpeeled potatoes in boiling, salted water. Drain well and peel them as soon as they can be handled. Put the potatoes through a mouli or push them through a coarse sieve while they are still warm. Put the potato purée in a mixing bowl. Sift in most of the flour and knead, adding more flour if necessary to the mixture, which should be soft, smooth and still slightly sticky to the touch.

Shape the dough into sausage-shaped rolls and cut them into 2.5 cm/1 inch lengths. Roll each piece of dough over the tines of a fork to give it the characteristic gnocchi finish. Set the gnocchi aside until you are ready to cook them.

TO MAKE THE SAUCE: place the cream in a small heavy-bottomed saucepan over a moderate heat. Bring it to the boil and continue to heat until it is reduced by half. Add the broad beans and sage, reduce the heat and simmer the sauce for 2-3 minutes.

TO COOK AND SERVE THE GNOCCHI: bring a large saucepan of water to the boil, drop in the gnocchi a few at a time and simmer for 5

Gnocchi with Prosciutto and Broad Beans needs only salad to complement.

minutes. They will rise to the surface of the pan when they are cooked. Lift them out with a slotted spoon and place in a warm, buttered serving dish.

When they are all cooked, ladle over the cream and broad bean mixture. Scatter over the prosciutto, salt and pepper and serve immediately, handing the Parmesan cheese in a separate serving bowl.

Accompany the gnocchi and their sauce with a salad of sliced tomatoes and freshly chopped basil.

PASTICCIO DI MACCHERONI ALLA FERRARESE

(Macaroni Pie Ferrara-style)

Originally intended for the tables of Italian nobility, this dish presents an intriguing combination of sophistication and simplicity. The meat sauce and the pastry can be made 1 day in advance.

SERVES 8-10

MEAT SAUCE:
2 tablespoons olive oil
½ onion, peeled and chopped finely
450 g/1 lb good-quality minced beef or
 veal
salt
1 truffle, chopped or 15 g/½ oz dried
 porcini mushrooms, soaked in warm
 water for 45 minutes, drained and
 sliced finely

PASTRY:
500 g/1¼ lb plain flour
175 g/6 oz sugar
300 g/11 oz butter, softened
4 egg yolks
beaten egg, to glaze

BÉCHAMEL SAUCE:
100 g/4 oz butter
pinch of salt
25 g/1 oz plain flour
1 litre/1¾ milk
2-3 tablespoons freshly grated Parmesan
 cheese

PIE FILLING:
300 g/11 oz macaroni
25 g/1 oz butter
25 g/1 oz prosciutto, sliced thinly
1 tablespoon freshly grated Parmesan
 cheese (optional)

A crisp and golden crust encases Pasticcio di Maccheroni alla Ferrarese.

TO MAKE THE MEAT SAUCE: heat the olive oil in a heavy-bottomed saucepan set over a moderate heat. Add the onion and fry for a few minutes until soft. Add the meat and fry until light brown. Reduce the heat, add salt and just enough cold water to cover. Cover the pan and simmer slowly for at least 1 hour. Add a little extra water if necessary. Add the truffle or mushrooms to the meat mixture about 10 minutes before the end of the cooking time.

TO MAKE THE PASTRY: put the flour and sugar on a large board and rub in the butter with your fingertips. Make a well in the centre, pour in the egg yolks and combine to make a rich dough. Form the dough into a ball. Do not handle the pastry too much or it will become tough. Wrap the dough in foil and refrigerate until it is required.

TO MAKE THE BÉCHAMEL SAUCE: melt the butter with the salt in a small, heavy pan over a moderate heat. Add all the flour at once, stir well and cook for 1 minute. Slowly pour in the milk, still stirring. Increase the heat and continue to stir with a wooden spoon as the sauce thickens and comes to the boil. Whisk well if necessary to disperse any lumps. Add the Parmesan cheese and check for seasoning. Set aside to keep warm while you cook the pasta.

TO COOK THE MACARONI: cook the pasta in a large pan of boiling salted water until it is *al dente*. Drain well and toss with butter to prevent the macaroni sticking together. Add the macaroni to the béchamel sauce, stirring well to coat the pasta thoroughly.

TO MAKE THE PIE: heat the oven to 180°C/350°F/Gas Mark 4. Cut the pastry into 2 pieces, one slightly larger than the other. Roll out the smaller piece to cover a 30 cm/12 inch pizza dish, allowing a 2 cm/¾ inch overlap all round. On this base place a layer of macaroni in sauce, a layer of meat sauce, strips of prosciutto and Parmesan cheese, if used. Repeat the layers. Roll out the remaining pastry into a large circle and place it carefully across the top of the pie. Close the edges by doubling the two layers of pastry and pinching a border all round. Roll out the pastry scraps and form them into leaves and flowers, or star shapes, to decorate the top of the pie. Brush with beaten egg to glaze.

Place on the centre shelf of the oven and bake for about 45 minutes, or until the pastry is well-cooked, crisp and golden brown.

TO SERVE: this dish is fairly substantial, but may be followed by a green salad and a salad of tomatoes, basil and green beans.

LIGHT RICE DISHES

ASPARAGUS RISOTTO

SERVES 4-6

225 g/8 oz asparagus, trimmed
50 g/2 oz unsalted butter
2 large shallots, finely chopped
salt and freshly ground black pepper
4 tablespoons dry white wine
200 g/7 oz Arborio rice
600-750 ml/1-1¼ pints chicken stock,
* simmering*
40 g/1½ oz grated Parmesan cheese
2 tablespoons chopped fresh parsley

Cut the tips from the asparagus and reserve them. Chop the stems into 1 cm/½ inch pieces and reserve these also.

Melt 50 g/2 oz of the butter in a large heavy frying pan and sauté the shallots until golden (about 5 minutes). Add the asparagus stems and season. Cook for 1 minute. Pour in the wine and cook, stirring constantly, until almost all the liquid has evaporated. Stir the rice into the pan and add 250 ml/8 fl oz of the chicken stock. Stir once. Cook without stirring, uncovered, over a medium to low heat, until the stock is absorbed. This should take about 10 minutes – if the liquid is being absorbed at a faster rate, reduce the heat. Pour 250 ml/8 fl oz more stock over the rice. Cook, without stirring, for 10 minutes longer. Stir the reserved asparagus tips into the rice. Add 120 ml/8 fl oz of the stock and cook until the liquid is absorbed and the rice is tender (about 8 more minutes). (If the rice is not tender at this point, add more stock. If it is too wet, turn up the heat slightly until the liquid is absorbed.) Stir in the remaining butter and the cheese.
TO SERVE: sprinkle with parsley.

MUSHROOM AND PECAN BROWN RICE SALAD

SERVES 6-8

450 g/1 lb brown rice (cooked
* according to Method 3 on page 15)*
100 g/4 oz mushroom caps, cleaned
* and sliced thinly*
1 sweet red or green pepper,
* chopped*
4 spring onions, chopped
2 stalks celery, chopped
50 g/2 oz pecan nuts, chopped
salt and freshly ground black pepper
2 tablespoons chopped parsley
1 medium tomato, peeled, seeded and
* diced*

DRESSING:
175 ml/6 fl oz olive oil
4 tablespoons white wine vinegar
salt
freshly ground black pepper
1 clove garlic, peeled and chopped
* finely*
1 tablespoon smooth peanut butter
2 teaspoons sesame seeds, lightly
* toasted*
120 ml/4 fl oz stir-fry sweet and sour
* sauce*

Place all the salad ingredients in a large serving bowl and fork together to combine lightly but thoroughly.
TO MAKE THE DRESSING: place all the ingredients in a food processor or blender and work to a smooth consistency. Alternatively, place the ingredients in a mixing bowl and whisk to combine them well.
TO SERVE: pour the dressing over the salad and toss it well. Leave in a cool place for up to 30 minutes so the flavours blend.

Accompany with a simple crisp green salad tossed in a vinaigrette dressing.

RISOTTO CON MELONE

(Risotto with Melon)

SERVES 4

100 g/4 oz butter
1 small onion, chopped finely
450 g/1 lb Arborio rice
salt
freshly ground black pepper
150 ml/¼ pint dry white wine
2 litres/3½ pints chicken stock
50 g/2 oz freshly grated Parmesan cheese
a few drops of Tabasco sauce
1 small very ripe cantaloup melon, peeled,
* seeded and diced (reserve juice)*

Melt half the butter in a large, heavy flame-proof casserole. Add the onion and cook over a moderate heat for 3-5 minutes until the onion is soft and golden. Add the rice, salt and pepper and stir with a wooden fork until the fork is completely covered with the mixture. Add the wine and cook until it is absorbed. Add the stock, 250 ml/8 fl oz at a time, stirring frequently until the rice absorbs the liquid. Keep the consistency creamy and, after about 15 minutes, test the rice. It must be *al dente*, not soft and mushy.

When the rice is cooked, remove it from the heat and stir in the remaining butter, the cheese and Tabasco sauce. Add the diced melon and juice. Transfer the risotto to a heated dish and allow to stand for a minute before serving.
TO SERVE: serve with warmed bread rolls and a salad of chicory.

Melon and Tabasco sauce provide texture and bite to counterbalance the creamy rice in Risotto con Melone.

ORIENTAL RICE

SERVES 6

500 g/1¼ lb long-grain rice
4 Chinese dried mushrooms, soaked in
   250 ml/8 fl oz water until tender
dash of soy sauce
dash of sesame oil
salt
pinch of sugar
1 egg white
2 teaspoons cornflour
175 g/6 oz boneless chicken, cubed
175 g/6 oz small shelled shrimps
2-3 tablespoons cooking oil
2 eggs, beaten lightly
1 tablespoon sherry
freshly ground black pepper
75 g/3 oz cooked peas
120 ml/4 fl oz hot chicken stock

GARNISH:
1 bunch spring onions, trimmed and
   chopped

Cook the rice according to one of the methods described on page 15. Let it stand for at least 1 hour.

Drain the mushrooms, reserving the liquid. Remove the stems from the mushrooms and cut the caps into 1 cm/½ inch squares. To the mushroom water add the soy sauce and sesame oil and a pinch each of salt and sugar.

Mix together the egg white and cornflour until blended and coat the chicken pieces and the shrimps with this mixture. Heat 1-2 tablespoons cooking oil in a frying pan over a low heat and fry the chicken and shrimps until they change colour. Set aside.

Add a little salt to the lightly beaten eggs. Heat 2 teaspoons of cooking oil in the frying pan. When it is hot, pour in the eggs and cook them quickly, stirring all the time.

Oriental Rice is teamed with Quick-fried Bean Sprouts and Water Chestnuts.

Remove from the pan and set aside.

Heat the remaining cooking oil in a wok over a moderate heat. Add the mushrooms, mushroom liquid, chicken and shrimps. Sprinkle with sherry and 1 teaspoon of salt, and stir-fry for 1 minute.

Mix in the cooked rice, and add a little pepper. Add the peas and scrambled eggs. Increase the heat and mix all the ingredients together for 2-3 minutes. Stir in the chicken stock, garnish with spring onions and serve immediately.

TO SERVE: this is a good partner for Quick-fried Bean Sprouts and Water Chestnuts (see recipe right).

QUICK-FRIED BEAN SPROUTS AND WATER CHESTNUTS

SERVES 6

3 tablespoons chicken fat
1 tablespoon chopped spring onions or
   chives
1 tablespoon chopped 'snow' pickled
   cabbage
500 g/1¼ lb bean sprouts
1×227 g/8 oz can water chestnuts,
   drained
1 teaspoon salt
3 tablespoons chicken broth or good stock
1 teaspoon sesame oil

Heat the chicken fat in a large saucepan over a high heat. Add the onions and pickled cabbage. Stir-fry for 30 seconds. Add the bean sprouts. Turn and stir-fry briskly until all the sprouts are well coated with fat. Add the water chestnuts. Sprinkle with salt, and continue to stir-fry for 1½ minutes. Add the chicken broth and sesame oil. Stir-fry for a minute more to heat through, and serve.

TO SERVE: accompany with Oriental Rice (see recipe left).

ORIENTAL FLAIR

Using a few distinctively Oriental ingredients, a number of far more familiar items can be transformed — with rice as the basis — into an Asian feast. Imaginative presentation is important: choose appropriate dishes and chopsticks and serve fragrant teas in porcelain cups.

POUSSINS WITH RICE AND MUSHROOM FILLING

SERVES 4

4×400 g/14 oz oven-ready poussins
175 g/6 oz butter for roasting
salt
freshly ground black pepper

FILLING:
100 g/4 oz long-grain rice
15 g/½ oz butter
75 g/3 oz button mushrooms, sliced
50 g/2 oz diced cooked ham, including
*   some fat*

SAUCE:
500 ml/18 fl oz chicken or veal stock
1 tablespoon rice filling (see above)

TO MAKE THE FILLING: cook the rice according to one of the methods described on page 15. Place the cooked rice in a mixing bowl.

Melt the butter in a small saucepan over a moderate heat and fry the mushrooms briefly. Add them to the rice. Sauté the ham for 2-3 minutes until the fat frizzles a little. Add pepper, toss with a fork and taste for salt. Add the ham to the rice mixture.

TO COOK THE POUSSINS: heat the oven to 190°C/375°F/Gas Mark 5. Clean the poussins and pat dry with paper towels. Fill the cavity of each bird with the rice mixture, reserving 1 tablespoon for the sauce. Pull the skin down over the opening and secure firmly with 1 or 2 poultry pins.

Lightly butter a roasting pan. Stand the birds in the pan and season them well. Melt the remaining butter and pour it over. Cook on the centre shelf of the oven for 45-50 minutes. Transfer the birds to a plate and keep warm in the turned-off oven while making the sauce.

TO MAKE THE SAUCE: pour all the fat from the roasting pan. Add the stock to the sediment in the pan. Add the reserved rice filling and reduce quickly over a high heat until 250 ml/8 fl oz of liquid remains. Strain into a heated bowl, pressing on the mixture with a wooden spoon so that some rice purée will go through and thicken the sauce. Taste for seasoning.

TO SERVE: place one poussin on each plate with a little sauce spooned around it. Serve with lightly steamed broccoli.

KOULIBIAC

(Russian Fish Pie)

SERVES 8

1×480 g/15 oz can red salmon
100 g/4 oz long-grain rice
40 g/1½ oz butter
15 g/½ oz flour
2 teaspoons tomato purée
225 g/8 oz mushrooms, chopped
4 hard-boiled eggs, shelled and chopped
2 tablespoons freshly chopped parsley
juice of 1 lemon
salt
freshly ground black pepper
2×212 g/7½ oz packets puff pastry
1 beaten egg, to glaze

Drain the salmon and retain all the juice. Remove and discard the skin and bones. Place the flesh in a large bowl and break it up with a fork.

Cook the rice according to one of the methods described on page 15 and leave to cool slightly.

Melt 15 g/½ oz butter in a small saucepan set over a low heat. Stir in the flour to make a smooth purée. Cook for 1 minute, stirring constantly. Add the salmon juice and tomato purée. Increase the heat and bring the sauce to the boil, still stirring. Let it cook for 1-2 minutes and remove the saucepan from the heat.

Melt the remaining butter in a saucepan and quickly fry the chopped mushrooms. Add them to the salmon with the rice, eggs and parsley. Mix in the sauce and lemon juice and season to taste. Set aside and leave to cool.

Heat the oven to 230°C/450°F/Gas Mark 8.

Take 1 packet of pastry and cut off a little to make decorations. Roll out the remainder to a fish or oblong shape to form the base of the pie and place it on a greased baking tray. Pile the mixture on top, leaving a margin of 5 cm/2 inches all around. Brush the edge of the pastry base with beaten egg. Roll out the second packet of pastry to a fish or oblong shape slightly larger than the base and place it on top. Fold the edges of the base and lid together and pinch them firmly. Make a small incision in the top of the pie to allow steam to escape while it is cooking. Decorate the centre with pastry shapes and brush the top all over with beaten egg so that it will brown nicely.

Place the pie in the oven and bake for 10 minutes. Reduce the heat to 200°C/400°F/Gas Mark 6 and continue to cook for a further 25 minutes. Serve hot, directly from the baking tray, as the pie will be quite fragile and require careful handling.

TO SERVE: this dish really needs no accompaniment, but if you wish to serve a vegetable, try sweetcorn kernels, perhaps tossed in a little butter.

PRAWNS WITH BROWN RICE

SERVES 4

400 g/14 oz brown rice
salt
225 g/8 oz toasted pine nuts
4 tablespoons freshly chopped parsley
1 kg/2 lb Mediterranean prawns, cooked, peeled, cleaned and cut in large chunks
600 ml/1 pint single cream
200 g/7 oz freshly grated or desiccated coconut
freshly ground black pepper

To cook the rice, follow Method 3 described on page 15. Drain the cooked rice well and toss with the pine nuts and parsley.

Place the prawns in a saucepan with the cream, coconut and pepper to taste. Simmer over a low heat for 5-10 minutes.

TO SERVE: spoon the prawn mixture into the centre of a serving platter and surround with the flavoured rice. Accompany with a salad of chopped celery and baby mushrooms in a garlic-flavoured vinaigrette.

KEDGEREE

SERVES 4

225 g/8 oz smoked haddock fillet
225 g/8 oz long-grain rice
100 g/4 oz butter, melted
1 hard-boiled egg, chopped
freshly ground black pepper

GARNISH:
1 hard-boiled egg, sliced
2 tablespoons freshly chopped parsley

To cook the fish, place it in a shallow pan and just cover it with cold water. Bring the

Fresh coconut adds flavour and flair to Prawns with Brown Rice.

water to the boil over a moderate heat. Reduce the heat and poach the fish for 4-5 minutes. Drain well, remove the skin and flake the flesh.

Cook the rice according to one of the methods on page 15. Drain the cooked rice well and fork in the fish. Add the butter, chopped egg and pepper to taste and toss with a fork lightly to mix all the ingredients evenly together.

TO SERVE: pile the kedgeree onto a warm serving platter, garnish with slices of hard-boiled egg and sprinkle with chopped parsley. This dish is usually served on its own.

JAVANESE CHICKEN

SERVES 6

250 ml/8 fl oz coconut milk (see method)
1 tablespoon oil
2 large onions, peeled and diced
1.5 kg/3 lb chicken pieces
1 teaspoon salt
2 teaspoons ground turmeric
2 teaspoons freshly grated ginger
2 teaspoons ground coriander
1 teaspoon ground cumin
4 cloves garlic, peeled and crushed
4 medium tomatoes, peeled and chopped
3 chillies, seeded and chopped finely
   (optional)
1 teaspoon grated or powdered laos
1 tablespoon lemon juice
1 tablespoon desiccated coconut, toasted
   lightly
1 piece lemon grass or 1×7.5 cm/3 inch
   piece lemon rind
2 cinnamon sticks

Make the coconut milk following the instructions given under Nasi Lemak on page 86 but using 75 g/3 oz coconut and 250 ml/8 fl oz water.

Heat 1 tablespoon of oil in a large saucepan over a moderate heat. Fry the onions until soft. Lift from the pan and set aside. Fry the chicken in the remaining oil until browned all over. Remove from the heat.

Place the salt, spices, garlic, tomatoes, chillies (if used), laos, coconut milk and lemon juice in a blender and blend until smooth. Pour the mixture into a large, heavy-bottomed pan. Stir in the toasted coconut and fried onion. Add to the chicken pieces with the lemon grass or rind and cinnamon sticks, stirring thoroughly. Cover the pan and set over a low heat. Simmer for 45 minutes, or until the chicken is tender.
TO SERVE: serve with Turmeric Rice.

TURMERIC RICE

SERVES 6

1 litre/1¾ pints coconut milk (see method)
425 g/15 oz long-grain rice
2 teaspoons turmeric
24 black peppercorns
6 crushed cardamom pods
2 tablespoons cooking oil
1 tablespoon butter
chopped chives, to garnish

Make the coconut milk following the instructions given under Nasi Lemak on page 86 but using 175 g/6 oz coconut and 1 litre/1¾ pints boiling water.

Wash the rice well in cold running water. Drain it thoroughly and place in a large heavy saucepan with all the other ingredients. Cover the pan and set it over a moderate heat. Bring the rice to the boil. Stir once, reduce the heat and cover the pan again. Leave to cook for 12-15 minutes, or until the rice is tender.
TO SERVE: transfer to a warmed serving bowl and garnish with chives.

CHICKEN PILAF

SERVES 4

75 g/3 oz butter
6 chicken thighs, trimmed of all fat
2 onions, peeled and sliced
200 g/7 oz long-grain rice
75 g/3 oz raisins
2 cardamom pods
1 bay leaf
1 teaspoon turmeric
900 ml/1¾ pints water or chicken stock
¼ teaspoon cloves
¼ teaspoon cinnamon
salt and freshly ground black pepper

Melt the butter in a large, heavy frying pan over a moderate heat. Fry the chicken and onions for a few minutes until they are golden. Add the rice, raisins, cardamom pods, bay leaf and turmeric and stir to coat them with the buttery mixture.

Place the water or stock in a saucepan and bring to the boil. Add the cloves and cinnamon and season with salt and pepper.

Pour the liquid over the chicken and rice and mix together lightly. Cover the pan, reduce the heat and simmer the mixture gently for about 25 minutes or until the rice and chicken are tender.
TO SERVE: serve with freshly tossed green salad as a contrast in texture.

STORE-CUPBOARD STANDBYS

Last-minute meals must often be produced when guests arrive unexpectedly. The well-prepared cook will always have rice in the store cupboard (as well as various pastas), knowing that it is one of the most versatile and nutritious standbys. Other essentials to have on hand: canned fish such as tuna, anchovies, shrimps and mussels, tomato purée, soy sauce, Tabasco, jars of capers, cornichons and olives, and dried mushrooms, as well as herbs and spices. Add the makings of a good salad — fresh, crisp vegetables with the best olive oil, lemons, salt and freshly ground black pepper for a dressing — and, with a little imagination and expertise, you have all the ingredients for a quick and delicious light lunch (or informal dinner).

TIMBALLO DI RISO

(Neapolitan Rice Timbale)

Bocconcini cheese is available seasonally in Britain (usually in the winter months). Mascarpone is an acceptable substitute – choose the plain rather than liqueur-flavoured variety.

SERVES 6

425 g/15 oz Arborio rice

SAUCE:
*1 kg/2 lb fresh tomatoes, peeled or canned
    peeled tomatoes, drained
2 tablespoons olive oil
4 fresh basil leaves
salt and freshly ground black pepper*

MEATBALLS:
*150 g/5 oz lean minced beef
1 egg, beaten
1 slice white bread, softened with 1
    tablespoon milk
salt and freshly ground black pepper
olive oil for frying*

FILLING:
*100 g/4 oz fresh bocconcini cheese,
    cubed
100 g/4 oz provolone cheese, cubed
4 thin Italian sausages
375 g/13 oz fresh shelled peas
100 g/4 oz butter
150 g/5 oz chicken livers, chopped
salt and freshly ground black pepper
2 hard-boiled eggs, sliced*

TO ASSEMBLE THE TIMBALE:
*15 g/½ oz butter
50 g/2 oz soft fresh breadcrumbs
100 g/4 oz grated Parmesan cheese
2 eggs, beaten*

Neapolitan in origin, Timballo di Riso is appetising either hot or cold.

Boil the rice in a large saucepan of salted water for 12 minutes. Drain and set aside.
TO MAKE THE SAUCE: place the tomatoes in a saucepan and crush them with a mallet or potato masher. Add the olive oil and basil leaves, and season to taste. Simmer slowly for about 30 minutes. Set aside.
TO MAKE THE MEATBALLS: mix together the minced beef, beaten egg, bread, salt and pepper and shape into very small balls. Heat the oil in a frying pan over a moderate heat and fry them quickly a few at a time. Drain on paper towels and set aside.
TO MAKE THE FILLING: combine the two varieties of cheese and set aside. Puncture the sausages with a small pin and place them in a saucepan. Cover with cold water and bring to the boil over a moderate heat. Simmer until the liquid evaporates, and allow the sausages to brown. Cut them into small pieces and set aside.

Place the peas in a small saucepan with 75 g/3 oz of the butter. Cover and cook over a moderate heat, shaking the pan, until just tender. Remove from the pan and set aside. Place the chicken livers and the remaining butter in the pan, season with salt and pepper and fry until firm. Set aside.
TO ASSEMBLE AND COOK THE TIMBALE: heat the oven to 190°C/375°F/Gas Mark 5. Butter a round ovenproof dish at least 13 cm/5 in high and sprinkle with the breadcrumbs. Mix the rice with three-quarters of the tomato sauce, half the Parmesan cheese and the beaten eggs. Place half the rice mixture in the dish and cover with the meatballs. Add a layer of half the mixed cheeses, then a layer of sausage pieces and spoon over 2 tablespoons of the remaining sauce. Cover with half the remaining rice mixture, a layer of peas, sautéed chicken livers, the remaining cubed cheese and a layer of sliced eggs. Cover with the remaining rice mixture and spoon over the remaining sauce. Sprinkle with the remaining Parmesan.
  Bake the timbale for approximately 1 hour or until golden brown. Remove from oven and leave to rest for 15 minutes. Unmould on to a large round platter.
TO SERVE: serve hot or cold with a simple green salad.

SALMON AND CUCUMBER MOULDS

Make individual rice moulds for a summer lunch, mixing diced cucumber with lightly lemon-flavoured rice and encircling each one with slivers of smoked salmon. Garnish with feathery sprigs of dill.

STUFFED WHITE CABBAGE WITH MEAT AND RICE

SERVES 6

12 leaves white cabbage
400 g/14 oz beef, minced
75 g/3 oz long-grain rice
salt
freshly ground black pepper

SAUCE:
4 tomatoes, peeled and chopped
1 carrot, peeled and cut into julienne
100 g/4 oz beetroot, cooked, peeled and
*   chopped*
2 tablespoons freshly chopped dill

Dip the leaves of cabbage quickly in boiling water and then in cold water to make them pliable. Dry them thoroughly on tea towels and spread out on a flat surface. Mix together the meat and rice, season with salt and pepper and divide the mixture evenly between the cabbage leaves. Roll up each one to form a parcel and secure with fine string. Place them side by side in 1 or 2 layers in a heavy saucepan.

TO MAKE THE SAUCE: place the tomatoes, carrot, beetroot and dill in a large saucepan with salt and pepper, and cook over a moderate heat for 10 minutes.

Spoon the sauce over the cabbage rolls, add 2 tablespoons of water and cover the pan tightly. Cook over a low heat until the meat and rice are cooked (at least 1 hour). If necessary, add a little extra water during the cooking time.

TO SERVE: if you wish to provide an accompaniment try side dishes of crisp salad or raw vegetables, as for Rice-stuffed Leeks (see recipe right).

RICE-STUFFED LEEKS

SERVES 4

8-10 medium-sized dried apricots
2 large leeks
2-3 tablespoons oil
juice of 1 lemon

STUFFING:
50 g/2 oz uncooked short-grain rice
1 medium onion
225 g/8 oz minced lamb
3 tablespoons chopped parsley
1 tablespoon crushed dried mint
salt
freshly ground black pepper

Pour boiling water over the apricots and leave them to soak for about 10 minutes.

Make the stuffing. Wash the rice thoroughly and drain it. Grate the onion. Mix the minced lamb with the rice, onion, chopped parsley, crushed mint and salt and pepper to taste. Knead the mixture thoroughly until smooth and set aside.

Discard any discoloured outer leaves from the leeks and cut off the untidy tops and solid bases. With a very sharp knife, cut each leek open lengthways to the centre. Open out the leaves and wash thoroughly in cold water.

Drain the apricots, reserving the soaking liquid. Chop the apricots very finely. Chop the small, innermost leaves of the leeks very finely and mix with the apricots. Add a couple of tablespoons of this mixture to the stuffing and reserve the rest.

Choose a large, heavy-bottomed saucepan that will hold all the stuffed leeks in a single layer, or two layers at the most. Chop the coarse outer leaves of the leeks and line the pan with them. Cut the rest of the leaves into 5 cm/2 inch lengths. Fill each leaf with a small, sausage-shaped roll of the filling

slightly shorter than the cut section of leaf, and wrap it up to make a roll (rather like cannelloni). With those pieces of leaf too small to go around the filling, close one piece partly around the filling, then put another piece on the other side to completely cover it. The curl of the leaf will keep the package together. (Blanch the stiff outer leaves for 1-2 minutes in boiling water, to make them more pliable.)

Gently fry the rolls of leek in a little oil in a frying pan, taking care that they do not unravel – which is easier than you might think. When they are golden, transfer them to the saucepan, packing them closely and neatly with the larger rolls in the centre.

Pour away any oil left in the frying pan and add the leek and apricot mixture. Cook quickly on a fairly high heat, stirring constantly, for a minute or so; then add the apricot-soaking water, salt, pepper, and lemon juice. Pour this mixture over the leeks in the saucepan; they should be just covered.

Set the pan on the stove, bring to the boil, and reduce the heat to simmer. Cover the leeks with an upturned plate wrapped in foil, put on a tight-fitting lid and leave to cook for 30-45 minutes. Check from time to time that the liquid is not evaporating too quickly; it should have reduced to a good thick sauce by the time the leeks and filling are cooked. If it isn't thick enough, reduce quickly with the lid off the pan.

TO SERVE: serve warm or cold, with a simple, refreshing salad or side dishes of little savouries (olives, gherkins, baby onions or crudités) to provide a contrast in texture.

CHAPTER FIVE

ENTERTAINING

Rice and pasta served with elegance,
perfect solutions for those special occasions

Once upon a time the word entertaining conjured up pictures of formal dinner parties, engraved invitations and a strict attention to etiquette that somehow seemed to override the importance of the food, the wine and the guests. Today, entertaining has a welcome spontaneity and an air of relaxation, which means a memorable time for guests and hosts alike.

Advance planning is the key to success, from the selection of appropriate table linen and tableware to the candles, flowers and any special accessories, such as ribbons to decorate table napkins. The menu should be arranged several days ahead of time, always including fresh seasonal ingredients that are chosen with care and combined with imagination. The inspiration may be seafood, young lamb or asparagus but, whatever the key element, select flavours and textures that balance and enhance each other.

It is to be hoped, of course, that your guests will contribute to the occasion with their conversation and wit. This can be encouraged with a selection of good wines. By all means follow the rules of white before red, dry before sweet, young before old, but don't shy from breaking with tradition on occasion. Some light red wines are marvellous with fish, some full-flavoured whites perfect with the main meat course, so enjoy experimenting.

Maintain your style to the end of the meal. Your contented guests will relax and enjoy the very best coffee or fragrant tea, or perhaps a choice of fine brandy or liqueurs – and so will you. Today entertaining means enjoyment for everyone concerned.

Entertaining no longer dictates formality and grandeur but special occasions provide a perfect excuse to show off your best crystal, china and silver. Whether you prefer the traditional approach using classic pieces or a more avant-garde table setting, make sure you don't neglect the fine detail – here, crisp napkins and fresh flowers complete the picture.

MENU FOR SIX

Avocado dip with crudités

FETTUCCINE WITH LOBSTER SAUCE

Strawberry shortcake

▼

Wine: Australian or New Zealand
Sauvignon Blanc

FETTUCCINE WITH LOBSTER SAUCE

2 lobsters, freshly cooked and heads
removed
1 tablespoon butter
1 large clove garlic, peeled and chopped
1 green pepper, diced
4 spring onions, chopped
salt
freshly ground black pepper
600 ml/1 pint single cream
750 g/1½ lb fettuccine

GARNISH:
sprigs of dill

Split the lobsters. Crack open the legs, removing the central membrane, and retain them for a garnish. Remove all the meat from the shells and chop evenly.

Melt the butter in a frying pan over a moderate heat. Gently cook the lobster and garlic for 5 minutes, stirring occasionally. Add the green pepper and spring onions, and continue to cook for a further 5 minutes

or until the vegetables have begun to soften. Season to taste and stir in the cream. Increase the heat and bring just to the boil. Reduce the heat and simmer so that the flavours amalgamate well and the sauce reduces slightly. Do not overcook, or the lobster will toughen.

Meanwhile, cook the fettuccine in a large saucepan of boiling salted water until it is *al dente*. Drain well and divide between individual warmed dishes. Spoon the lobster sauce over the pasta. Garnish with the lobster legs and sprigs of dill.

MENU FOR FOUR

Artichokes vinaigrette

SEAFOOD CANNELLONI

Salad of fennel and watercress

Caramelized oranges

▼

Wine: Italian Soave Classico

SEAFOOD CANNELLONI

PASTA:
425 g/15 oz plain flour
4 large eggs, beaten
pinch of salt

FILLING:
2 tablespoons finely chopped onion
4 tablespoons olive oil
450 g/1 lb shelled and cleaned uncooked
prawns, chopped finely
salt and freshly ground white pepper

120 ml/4 fl oz dry Italian vermouth
2×425 g/15 oz cans Italian tomatoes,
drained and chopped
1 teaspoon chopped fresh oregano
small sprig of rosemary
30 mussels, removed from the shells

TO COOK THE CANNELLONI:
100 g/4 oz freshly grated Parmesan cheese
50 g/2 oz soft butter

TO MAKE THE PASTA: make the dough as described on page 10. Turn it on to a floured board and knead until it is smooth and elastic. Roll out by hand to the correct thickness or put the dough through the thickest roller of a pasta maker. Cut in rectangles about 10×15 cm/4×6 inches, and cover.
TO MAKE THE FILLING: sauté the onion in the oil until soft but not brown. Add the prawns, salt and pepper and sauté for a few minutes. Remove the prawns and set aside. Pour the vermouth into the pan and, over a high heat, reduce to about 2 tablespoons. Add the tomatoes, oregano and rosemary and cook over a high heat until the sauce has thickened. Add the mussels and prawns and set aside. Remove the rosemary.
TO MAKE AND COOK THE CANNELLONI: heat the oven to 190°C/375°F/Gas Mark 5. Cook the pasta rectangles in a large saucepan of boiling salted water for 5-6 minutes. Drain in a colander, rinse under cold water and lay on a clean tea towel. Put some filling on one end of each rectangle. Sprinkle with cheese, roll up and press the ends together. Grease an ovenproof dish and place in the cannelloni side by side. Pour over any remaining juices from the sauce, sprinkle with the remaining cheese and dot with butter. Bake for 30-40 minutes or until golden brown.

Summery Fettuccine with Lobster Sauce
– perfect pasta for warmer weather.

MENU FOR FOUR

Antipasti misti

CRAB AND BASIL RAVIOLI

Ginger ice cream

Brandy snaps

▼

Wine: Australian

Hunter Valley Sémillon

CRAB AND BASIL RAVIOLI

COURT BOUILLON:
1 litre/1¾ pints dry white wine
1 carrot, peeled and sliced
1 onion, peeled and sliced
parsley
thyme
1.75 litres/3 pints water
6 tablespoons vinegar
coarsely ground pepper

RAVIOLI:
2×450-750 g/1-1½ lb crabs
salt
20 basil leaves
75 g/3½ oz butter
1 chilli, seeded and chopped finely
225 g/8 oz good fresh pasta dough
1 egg, beaten
1 tomato, peeled, seeded and diced
1 lemon

Combine all the ingredients for the court bouillon in a large saucepan and bring to the boil. Cook the crabs in the rapidly boiling liquid, remove and cool. Strain the bouillon, discarding solids, and reserve.

Shell the crabs. You should have about 300 g/11 oz of meat and coral. Add salt to taste, then mash the crab meat into a paste with 10 basil leaves and half the butter. Add chopped chilli to taste.

Roll out the dough and cut into 32 squares measuring 7.5 cm/3 inches. Place a spoonful of crab mixture on each square, brush a little beaten egg on the inside edges of the pastry and fold on the diagonal, pressing to seal the edges (make sure there are no air pockets).

To make the sauce, reduce 250 ml/8 fl oz of the reserved court bouillon and thicken it with the remaining butter. Add the remaining basil leaves, diced tomato and a dash of lemon juice. Adjust the seasoning.

Bring the remaining court bouillon to the boil. Add the ravioli and cook for 3-4 minutes. Drain, transfer to a serving dish and pour over the sauce.

MENU FOR FOUR

Asparagus with melted butter

OYSTER RAVIOLI WITH SCALLOPS AND

CHAMPAGNE SAUCE

Celery and cucumber salad

Monte Bianco (chestnut purée with

whipped cream)

▼

Wine: Champagne or a méthode

champenoise wine

OYSTER RAVIOLI WITH SCALLOPS AND CHAMPAGNE SAUCE

20 scallops, cleaned, with roe attached
plain flour for dusting
oil for frying

PASTA:
200 g/7 oz plain flour
2 large eggs
pinch of salt

FILLING:
16 shelled oysters

SAUCE:
1 carrot, peeled and diced
1 leek, cleaned and diced
4 shallots, peeled and diced
300 ml–½ pint champagne
7 tablespoons crème fraîche
100 g/4 oz butter
salt
freshly ground black pepper

GARNISH:
chopped parsley

TO MAKE THE RAVIOLI: make the dough in a food processor as described on page 10. Roll out by hand or machine to give 4 strips or 2 large thin pasta sheets. Leave to dry for 15 minutes.

Place the oysters at equal intervals along 2 of the strips or 1 of the sheets. The finished ravioli should be about 7.5 cm/3 inches square. Place the remaining pasta on top, brush one edge to seal, and cut out the ravioli with a pastry cutter. Fold over the edges firmly to make neat airtight parcels.

Bring a large saucepan of salted water to the boil. Add a dash of oil and cook the ravioli in the water for about 1 minute or until soft to the touch. Remove with a slotted spoon and place in a bowl of iced water.

Carefully drain the ravioli, toss in a little oil and set aside.

TO MAKE THE SAUCE: put the carrot, leek and shallots in a saucepan with the champagne. Bring to the boil and reduce by half. Add the crème fraîche and reduce by half again.

TO COOK THE SCALLOPS: dust them with flour and fry quickly in oil a few at a time, until they are brown and just cooked inside.

TO SERVE: whisk the butter into the sauce and season to taste.

Place 5 scallops in the centre of each warmed plate and arrange the ravioli around them. Pour the sauce over the ravioli and garnish with chopped parsley.

MENU FOR SIX

Parma ham with celeriac salad

LOBSTER MEDALLION ON NOODLES

Lemon sorbet

Langues de chat

▼

Wine: Australian, New Zealand or French Gewürztraminer

LOBSTER MEDALLION ON NOODLES WITH GINGER AND CORIANDER BUTTER

2 fresh lobster tails, shells removed and reserved
6 large green cabbage leaves
40 g/1½ oz butter

1 cm/½ inch piece fresh ginger, peeled and grated
2 tablespoons freshly chopped coriander
450 g/1 lb tomato-flavoured angel's hair pasta (see Pasta all'Uovo on page 10)
2 tablespoons pickled Japanese ginger, sliced

LOBSTER STOCK:
reserved lobster shells
4 shallots, peeled
2 cloves garlic, peeled
1 carrot, peeled and chopped
2 sprigs parsley
1 litre/1¾ pints water

SAUCE:
350 ml/12 fl oz single cream
1 teaspoon saffron strands, soaked in 1 tablespoon warm water for 30 minutes
salt and freshly ground white pepper

GARNISH:
2 tablespoons salmon roe
sprigs of fresh coriander

TO MAKE THE LOBSTER PARCELS: cut the lobster into 6 equal medallions.

Blanch the cabbage leaves in boiling salted water. The moment they turn a bright green colour, remove them from the pan and refresh in a bowl of iced water.

Place each medallion of lobster on a cabbage leaf with ½ tablespoon of butter and a pinch of freshly grated ginger and chopped coriander on top. Wrap up the leaves to make parcels and leave in the refrigerator.

TO MAKE THE LOBSTER STOCK: place the lobster shells, shallots, garlic, carrot and parsley in a saucepan with the cold water and simmer over a low heat for 2 hours or until reduced by two-thirds. Strain off the liquid and set aside.

TO MAKE THE SAUCE: boil the cream until reduced by half. Add the lobster stock and

Oyster Ravioli with Scallops and Champagne Sauce – sublime seafood for a delicious late supper.

---

simmer for 15 minutes. Add the saffron in its liquid. Season with salt and white pepper.

TO COOK AND SERVE: steam the lobster parcels to heat them through gently without toughening the meat (about 8-20 minutes, depending on size).

Meanwhile, cook the pasta in a large saucepan of boiling water until it is *al dente*. Drain and toss in butter to glaze. Toss the pasta with the Japanese ginger and place on individual heated plates.

Place one lobster parcel in the centre of each plate, and spoon a little of the sauce on top. Garnish with salmon roe and sprigs of coriander. Serve immediately, handing the remaining sauce separately.

RAVIOLI OF DUCK WITH ASPARAGUS AND WATERCRESS SAUCE

PASTA:
300 g/11 oz plain flour
4 eggs
pinch of salt
flour for rolling out

FILLING:
2 breasts of duck, cooked and diced finely
25 g/1 oz soft white breadcrumbs
100 g/4 oz cooked chopped spinach
1-2 tablespoons butter
2-3 shallots, peeled and chopped
2-3 tablespoons single cream
salt and freshly ground black pepper
1 egg, beaten

SAUCE:
6 asparagus stems, chopped in 5 cm/
  2 inch lengths
100 g/4 oz broccoli florets
1 small bunch watercress, chopped finely
250 ml/8 fl oz hot chicken stock
120 ml/4 fl oz single cream
salt and freshly ground black pepper

TO MAKE THE PASTA: make the dough in a food processor as described on page 10. To roll it out, divide it into 4 pieces for ease of handling. If using a machine, roll to the finest setting. Dough rolled out by hand should be as fine as a piece of cloth. With a fluted pastry cutter, cut out about 60 circles of pasta each about 10 cm/4 inches in diameter. Leave the pasta to rest.

TO MAKE THE FILLING: combine the diced duck with the breadcrumbs and spinach in a mixing bowl. Melt the butter in a frying pan over a low heat and sauté the shallots. Remove the pan from the heat and add the duck mixture to the shallots, blending all together well. Add enough cream to moisten the mixture and season generously.

Place a heaped teaspoon of the filling on half of the pasta circles. Brush the edges with a little beaten egg to seal and place another circle of pasta on top. Pinch the edges together firmly. Leave the ravioli to stand on a floured tea towel for about 1 hour.

TO MAKE THE SAUCE: cook the asparagus in a saucepan of boiling salted water until just tender. Quickly drain it and refresh under cold running water. Cook the broccoli florets in the same way. Put the asparagus, broccoli, watercress, chicken stock and cream in a food processor or blender and purée. Alternatively press all three vegetables through a coarse sieve and stir into the chicken stock. Strain the stock into a saucepan and season to taste. Stir in the cream and set aside.

TO COOK AND SERVE THE RAVIOLI: bring 1 or 2 large saucepans of salted water to the boil and cook the ravioli for 4-5 minutes. Meanwhile, heat the sauce through and pour on to individual warmed dishes. Drain the cooked ravioli well and place 5-6 on each dish. Serve immediately.

WARM PASTA SALAD WITH QUAIL AND ABALONE

50 g/2 oz butter
4 dressed quail
4 rashers streaky bacon
2 abalone, trimmed
200 ml/⅓ pint walnut oil
1½ lemons
salt
freshly ground black pepper
100 g/4 oz vermicelli
1 sweet red pepper
50 g/2 oz dried black mushrooms, soaked in warm water for 30 minutes and drained
4 mignonette lettuce leaves
oil for frying

Heat the oven to 220°C/425°F/Gas Mark 7.
Place a 15 g/½ oz pat of butter inside each quail and wrap each one in a rasher of bacon. Place in a roasting pan and bake in the oven for 10 minutes until just cooked. The flesh should be tender but still pink.

Place the abalone in a plastic bag and beat with a meat mallet until thin. Cut into 1 cm/½ inch cubes.

Prepare a dressing by placing two-thirds of the walnut oil, the juice of 1 lemon and seasoning in a screwtop jar and shaking it well.

Cook the vermicelli in a large saucepan of boiling salted water until it is *al dente*. Drain and set aside.

To peel the sweet red pepper, toast it over a flame or under a hot grill until the skin is charred all over. Place it under cold water, remove the skin and cut the pepper into julienne. Mix together the pasta, red pepper strips and mushrooms and toss them with the dressing.

Separate the breast meat from the quail. Remove the legs and cut in two at the joints. Put these pieces in a mixing bowl and dribble the remaining walnut oil over them, turning them gently.

Place a lettuce leaf on each plate. Divide the pasta salad equally between the plates, and arrange the quail breasts and legs on top.

Heat a little oil in a frying pan and quickly fry the abalone until tender – about 1 minute. Squeeze the half lemon over them and season with salt and pepper. Arrange the abalone around the edge of the plates and serve immediately.

Warm Pasta Salad with Quail and Abalone entices the palate with its flavours.

SAFFRON PASTA

PASTA:
450 g/1 lb unbleached plain flour
5 extra large eggs
pinch of salt
1 scant teaspoon powdered saffron, or sachet saffron threads, finely ground with marble mortar and pestle

TO COOK THE PASTA:
sea salt
25 g/1 oz unsalted butter

SAUCE:
3 medium leeks, white parts only or 3 medium red onions, peeled
4 tablespoons olive oil
25 g/1 oz unsalted butter
1×4 cm/1½ inch slice of veal shank, with bone and marrow in the centre
1 tablespoon unbleached plain flour
½ medium red onion, peeled
1 small celery stalk
1 small carrot, scraped
1 small piece lemon rind
250 ml/8 fl oz dry white wine
12 canned tomatoes, drained

1 tablespoon tomato purée
salt
freshly ground black pepper

GARNISH:
1 large clove garlic, peeled
15 sprigs Italian parsley, leaves only
4 sage leaves, fresh or preserved in salt
grated peel of 1 lemon

Make the pasta by hand or with a pasta machine. Put the flour in a mound on a large board. Use a fork to make a well in the centre and put the eggs, salt and saffron in the well. Use the fork to mix together the eggs, salt and saffron, incorporating flour from the inner rim of well.

Start kneading the dough by hand to get an elastic ball of dough; finish kneading either by hand or with the rollers of the pasta machine. Stretch the pasta to a thickness of less than 1.5 mm/1⁄16 inch by hand, or with the pasta machine at the finest setting. Cut into tagliatelle – strips of pasta about 5 mm/¼ in wide.

Put the cut pasta on cotton tea towels to dry for 15 minutes, or until needed.

TO MAKE THE SAUCE: slice the leeks into rings about 1 cm/½ inch wide. Put the rings in a bowl of cold water and soak for 30 minutes or until all the sand is removed.

Heat the oil and butter in a flameproof casserole over a medium heat. When the butter is completely melted, drain the leeks and add them to the casserole. Sauté in the butter for 5 minutes.

Tie the veal shank with string all around the edge to keep it together. Lightly flour the veal on both sides. Add the meat to the casserole and sauté until it is golden brown on both sides (about 4 minutes on each side).

Meanwhile, finely chop the onion, celery, carrot and lemon rind together on a board. Add the chopped ingredients to the cas-serole and sauté for 2 minutes longer. Add the wine and let it evaporate over a low heat for 20 minutes. Add the whole tomatoes and tomato purée, cover the casserole, and simmer for 40 minutes, stirring occasionally. Taste for salt and pepper. Turn the veal shank, cover the casserole again, and simmer for 25 minutes longer. When it is cool enough, transfer the meat to a board and remove the string and bone.

Pass the casserole contents and meat through a food mill, using a disc with medium-sized holes, and into a second casserole. Simmer this sauce, uncovered, over a medium heat for about 15 minutes. Taste for salt and pepper. Once the sauce is ready, remove the casserole from the heat and let it stand, covered, until needed.

TO PREPARE THE GARNISH: finely chop the garlic, parsley and sage together on a board. Transfer the chopped ingredients to a small crockery or glass bowl. Add the grated lemon peel and mix all the ingredients together with a wooden spoon. Cover the bowl and let it stand until needed.

TO COOK AND SERVE: bring a large quantity of cold water to the boil and add sea salt to taste. Melt the butter on a large serving platter placed over boiling water. Meanwhile, reheat the sauce.

When the butter is melted, remove the platter and add the pasta to the salted boiling water. Cook for 40 seconds-1 minute, depending on the dryness of the pasta. Drain the pasta and transfer it to the serving platter with the melted butter. Pour the sauce over and toss very well. Sprinkle with the chopped herbs and lemon peel and serve immediately.

The pure luxury of walnut oil brings Buckwheat Pasta Salad to life.

MENU FOR SIX

Crab and sweetcorn soup

BUCKWHEAT PASTA SALAD WITH WALNUT VINAIGRETTE

Raspberry sorbet

Macaroons

▼

Wine: Californian Zinfandel

BUCKWHEAT PASTA SALAD

BUCKWHEAT PASTA:
100 g/4 oz buckwheat flour
200 g/7 oz plain flour
2 tablespoons chopped herbs, such as basil,
 sorrel, marjoram, chives, thyme and
 parsley
salt
3 teaspoons olive oil
3 large eggs

WALNUT VINAIGRETTE:
1 tablespoon walnut oil
3 tablespoons safflower oil
1 tablespoon white wine vinegar
salt
freshly ground black pepper

SALAD:
1 green pepper, cut in julienne
2 sweet red peppers, cut in julienne
2 medium cucumbers, cut in julienne

GARNISH:
fine slivers of truffle or mustard and cress
175 g/6 oz finely sliced smoked beef

Make the pasta in a food processor as described on page 10, using 1 teaspoon olive oil and incorporating the herbs with the flour. Cut to form fine noodles and leave to dry for 15-30 minutes.

To make the walnut dressing, whisk all the ingredients together vigorously or process in a blender.

Bring a large pan of salted water to the boil. Add the remaining 2 teaspoons of olive oil. Drop the pasta into the rapidly boiling water and boil for 3 minutes at a very high heat. Place in a colander and thoroughly rinse under running water. Shake well to drain the pasta.

Warm the walnut oil dressing and toss through the pasta noodles.

TO SERVE: toss the vegetables through the pasta, garnish with the truffle or mustard and cress, and surround with pale pink, very thin medallions of smoked beef.

POPPY SEED TAGLIATELLE WITH RABBIT, APPLE AND FRESH CHERVIL

PASTA:
350 g/12 oz plain flour
3 large eggs
1 tablespoon olive oil
pinch of salt
15 g/½ oz poppy seeds

SAUCE:
40 g/1½ oz butter
2 saddles of rabbit, sawn through in 2.5 cm/1 inch pieces, kidneys reserved
1 clove garlic, peeled and chopped (optional)
3 tablespoons white wine
250 ml/8 fl oz chicken stock or rabbit stock made from remaining carcass
4 sprigs fresh chervil or ½ teaspoon dried chervil
salt

freshly ground black pepper
2 tablespoons soured cream

CARAMELIZED APPLES:
25 g/1 oz butter
2 Granny Smith apples, peeled, cored and quartered
1 tablespoon brown sugar

GARNISH:
4 sprigs of chervil

Make the pasta by hand as described on page 10, incorporating the poppy seeds with the flour. Roll out by hand or machine until very fine and cut into narrow strips about 5 mm/¼ inch wide.

Melt the butter in a large heavy frying pan and cook the rabbit pieces and kidneys until golden on all sides. Add the garlic, if using, and cook until soft. Lift out the rabbit and set aside for a moment.

Increase the heat and pour the wine into the pan. Deglaze the pan, scraping up the caramelized pieces. Return the rabbit pieces and kidneys to the pan and pour in the stock. Add the chervil and season to taste. Simmer, covered, for about 30 minutes or until tender. Keep warm.

Melt 25 g/1 oz butter in a pan. Add the apple pieces, sprinkle with brown sugar and cook over a moderate heat until caramelized. Set aside and keep warm.

Bring a large saucepan of salted water to the boil. Add a little oil, toss in the tagliatelle and cook until *al dente*. Drain and keep warm while you finish the sauce.

Add the soured cream to the rabbit sauce and heat through gently.

TO SERVE: arrange the pasta on 4 large warmed plates. Spoon the rabbit and kidneys on top. Arrange the apple slices around the plates and pour over the sauce. Garnish the individual helpings with chervil sprigs and serve at once.

VENISON CHESTNUT LASAGNE

450 g/1 lb venison steaks, cut 2.5 cm/1 inch thick
1 tablespoon peanut oil
2 teaspoons butter
250 ml/8 fl oz game or beef stock
50 g/2 oz dried chestnuts, soaked overnight in water
1 medium carrot, peeled and sliced
1 stalk celery, sliced
8 spring onions, cleaned and trimmed

PASTA:
200 g/7 oz plain flour
2 eggs
50 g/2 oz chestnut purée
1 tablespoon oil

MARINADE:
1 small onion, peeled and sliced
1 small carrot, peeled and sliced
120 ml/4 fl oz white wine
2 tablespoons red wine vinegar
4 juniper berries
4 black peppercorns
1 sprig thyme
4 coriander seeds

Venison Chestnut Lasagne, the centrepiece for a perfectly presented dinner party.

SAUCE:
1 tablespoon redcurrant jelly
15 g/½ oz potato flour
1 tablespoon port
salt
freshly ground black pepper

<u>TO MAKE THE PASTA:</u> make the dough in a food processor as described on page 10, incorporating the chestnut purée with the eggs. Roll out in a machine or by hand to a fairly fine texture suitable for lasagne. Cut into sheets about 13×20 cm (5×8 inches). Leave the pasta to rest.

<u>TO MARINATE AND COOK THE VENISON:</u> combine the marinade ingredients and bring to the boil; pour over the steaks in a ceramic or glass dish. Turn the steaks, drizzle with half the oil, cover and leave to marinate for at least 2 hours or refrigerate overnight.

To cook the venison, drain off the marinade, and reserve. Heat the remaining oil and butter in a heavy, flameproof casserole and seal the steaks on both sides. Add the stock, marinade, chestnuts and vegetables and braise, covered, over a low heat until the steaks are just tender. Lift the steaks out and keep them warm.

<u>TO MAKE THE SAUCE:</u> strain the juices into a clean saucepan and reduce to 250 ml/8 fl oz. Beat in the jelly and thicken the sauce with the potato flour mixed with the port. Adjust the seasoning. Cut the venison into bite-sized pieces and moisten with the sauce.

<u>TO COOK THE PASTA:</u> cook the lasagne in a large pan of rapidly boiling water with a little oil added, until *al dente*. Arrange 1 sheet on each of 4 heated dinner plates.

<u>TO SERVE:</u> divide the venison equally between the plates, spooning it over the pasta. Garnish each serving with the chestnuts and vegetables and top each with a second sheet of lasagne. Serve immediately.

CHOOSING WINES

Ideally, when entertaining, a different wine should be served with each course. Champagne is the one wine which may be drunk throughout the evening from pre-dinner drinks to dessert. Remember that sherry is making a return to favour as an aperitif. If you have any doubts about which wine to serve, the general guidelines are: white before red, dry before sweet, young before old. But rules are made to be broken, so don't be afraid of departing from tradition. Serve a full-bodied Chardonnay with light meat if that is what you enjoy, or a refreshing Beaujolais with fish. Dessert wines have been making a comeback recently and the choice in this field is growing wider. In the end, however, it is your preference that counts. Wine is for enjoying.

MENU FOR SIX

Gazpacho

PAELLA

Orange bavarois

▼

Wine: Spanish white Rioja

PAELLA

CHICKEN MIXTURE:
3 tablespoons olive oil
1 medium chicken, cut into 8 pieces
4 chorizos (hot Spanish sausages),
  sliced
2 medium onions, peeled and
  chopped
3 large tomatoes, peeled and cut
  into 8 pieces
1 canned pimiento, sliced finely
1 green pepper, seeded
  and sliced finely
225 g/8 oz fresh peas, blanched and
  refreshed
225 g/8 oz ham, cut in chunks

SEAFOOD:
1 kg/2 lb fresh mussels, scrubbed
250 ml/8 fl oz dry white wine
2 tablespoons finely chopped onion
4 tablespoons finely chopped parsley
250 ml/8 fl oz water
1 kg/2 lb fresh king prawns, cooked
1 crab, cooked

Colourful Paella combines rice and fresh seafood with piquant Spanish flavours.

RICE:
½ teaspoon powdered saffron (or to taste)
2 chicken stock cubes
750 g/1½ lb long-grain rice
4 tablespoons olive oil
2 large cloves garlic, peeled and crushed

GARNISH:
freshly ground black pepper
1 canned pimiento, sliced finely
1 green pepper, seeded and sliced finely
24 black olives, stoned
4 tablespoons freshly chopped parsley

Heat the oven to 140°C/275°F/Gas Mark 1.
TO MAKE THE CHICKEN MIXTURE: heat 2 tablespoons of olive oil in a large flameproof casserole over a moderate heat and fry the chicken pieces until pale gold all over. Add the chorizos and cook for 5 more minutes until lightly browned. Remove the casserole from the heat.

Heat 1 tablespoon of olive oil in a medium saucepan over a moderate heat. Sauté the chopped onions with the pieces of tomato until the onion is transparent. Add them to the casserole and stir in with the sliced pimiento, green pepper, peas and ham. Transfer the casserole to the oven to keep it warm.

TO COOK THE SEAFOOD: discard any mussels that have opened. Place the wine, chopped onion, parsley and the water in a large frying pan. Cover the pan and set it over a high heat for 5 minutes. Add the mussels, replace the lid and steam them to open, shaking the pan occasionally. Any that have not opened after 10 minutes should be discarded. Remove the top half of the shell from the mussels and discard. Place the cooked mussels in a covered ovenproof dish and set aside. Reserve the cooking liquid separately.

Peel half the prawns, leaving the tails on. Leave the rest of the prawns whole.

Remove all the meat from the body of the crab, retaining the back shell for a garnish. Crack the claws. Add the prawns, crab meat and claws to the mussels, and place the casserole in the oven to keep warm.

TO COOK THE RICE: meanwhile, place a large saucepan of water over a high heat and stir in the saffron and chicken stock cubes, together with the reserved juice from the mussels. Wash the rice and drain it well. When the water comes to the boil, add the rice and cook as for the Risotto method on page 15.

Set the paella dish over a low heat and gently heat the olive oil with the crushed garlic. Drain the cooked rice well and transfer it to the paella dish, tossing it in the warm oil.

TO ASSEMBLE THE PAELLA: add the chicken mixture to the pan and combine it with the rice. Carefully arrange the seafood in and around the rice with the crab shell on top, the largest prawns clearly visible and the shells of the mussels sitting up.

TO SERVE: sprinkle over the black pepper, pimiento, green pepper, olives and parsley. Serve immediately.

MENU FOR EIGHT

Tomato salad with salami and black olives

RISOTTO AL FRUTTI DI MARE

Peaches in white wine

▼

*Wine: Australian
Hunter Valley Chardonnay*

RISOTTO AL FRUTTI DI MARE

(Seafood Risotto)

*4 spring onions, chopped finely
1 piece fresh ginger, about 2.5 cm/1 inch
　long, peeled and chopped finely
1 medium carrot, peeled and chopped
　finely
1 stalk celery, chopped finely
50 g/2 oz butter
450 g/1 lb Arborio rice
175 ml/6 fl oz white wine
1 litre/1¾ pints chicken stock (good-
　quality stock cubes can be used)
1 pinch saffron, diluted in a little warm
　water
2 heaped teaspoons tandoori powder
2 dozen opened oysters or 1 large jar
1.5 kg/3 lb uncooked prawns, peeled and
　deveined (reserve a few in shells to
　garnish)
750 g/1½ lb scallops
4 tablespoons single cream
90 g/3½ oz freshly grated Parmesan
　cheese
salt
freshly ground black pepper*

In a large frying pan, fry the spring onions, ginger, carrot and celery in the butter until translucent. Add the rice and cook briefly to coat the grains. Add the wine and the stock (120 ml/4 fl oz at a time) and, stirring constantly, cook until the rice has absorbed the fluid. (The quantity of stock needed for the risotto will depend on the quality of the rice and degree of cooking.)

Add the saffron, tandoori powder, the liquid from the oysters and more stock. Stir occasionally until the rice is nearly cooked. Add the prawns and scallops; mix carefully and cook until the prawns are pink and scallops translucent. (Do not overcook seafood or it will toughen and shrink.)

When the rice is *al dente*, remove it from the stove, and add the cream, Parmesan cheese and oysters. Taste for salt and pepper and leave to rest for a few minutes before serving. Garnish with a few cooked prawns in their shells.

Risotto al Frutti di Mare.

NASI LEMAK

(Coconut Rice)

175-250 g/6-9 oz desiccated coconut
4.5 litres/7½ pints boiling water
4-5 blades lemon grass tied in a knot
1 kg/2 lb Basmati rice

GARNISH:
coriander leaves

SIDE DISHES:
raw peanuts, deep fried in oil, served
warm
a little ikanbillis (dried salted fish)
cucumbers, freshly sliced
hard-boiled eggs, shelled and quartered
fresh chillies, seeded and chopped
1 bunch bok choy (Chinese chard)

Place the coconut in a bowl and pour 1 litre/1¾ pints of the boiling water over it. Let it stand for 10 minutes, then make the milk by pressing the mixture through a very fine strainer into a bowl. Add the coconut milk to the rest of the boiling water. Add the lemon grass and pour in the rice. Bring the liquid to the boil again and cook the rice for 12 minutes. Drain well, remove the lemon grass and fluff up the rice with a fork.

TO SERVE: place the rice in a large bowl and garnish with coriander leaves. Place each side dish in a small separate bowl around the rice dish. To cook the bok choy, boil it until muddy green in colour and the liquid has evaporated. Add a few drops of sesame oil and a little oily chicken stock.

PRAWN STIR-FRY

2-3 tablespoons vegetable oil
1.75 kg/4 lb prawns, peeled but tails left
on
1-2 fresh chillies, sliced thinly
1×5 cm/2 inch piece ginger root, peeled
and sliced
4-5 cloves garlic, peeled and sliced
¼ bunch coriander, chopped roughly,
including root
225 g/8 oz mange tout, topped, tailed
and strings removed
75 g/3 oz toasted sesame seeds
1 lime, sliced thinly
juice of 1 lime

GARNISH:
1 bunch spring onions, cut in slivers
lengthways
a few sprigs of coriander

Heat the oil in a wok. (Do not overfill the wok as this dish must be cooked over a high heat; too much at one time and it will not stir-fry but stew and spoil; use 2 woks if possible.) Throw everything into the smoking oil and toss for 1-2 minutes. Allow 2-3 prawns per person. Garnish with spring onions and coriander.

MALAYSIAN CURRIED CHICKEN

2 tablespoons vegetable oil
a few cardamom seeds, crushed
3-4 cloves garlic, chopped
1 chilli, sliced
4-6 teaspoons Malaysian curry powder
2 kg/4 lb chicken thighs, chopped into
small pieces
1 tablespoon tamarind paste
500 ml/18 fl oz – 750 ml/1¼ pints water

Heat the oil in a saucepan. Add the cardamom seeds and toss around. Add the garlic, chilli, curry powder and chicken. Fry for a few minutes to brown the chicken. Mix the tamarind paste with the water and pour over the chicken. Simmer for 35 to 45 minutes until the chicken is cooked and the fluid has reduced to about one-third its original amount.

A bowl of coconut rice provides the centrepiece for this traditional Malaysian meal. Integral accompaniments are (left to right): quartered hard-boiled eggs, tiny salt-dried fish (ikanbillis), Prawn Stir-Fry and Malaysian Curried Chicken. You may also like to serve bowls of extra chillies, sliced cucumber, bok choy (Chinese chard) and fast-fry peanuts to complete the feast.

SPICED ALMOND CHICKEN

8 small chicken breasts on bone, skin
removed
juice of 1½ lemons
2 teaspoons salt
1 teaspoon cayenne pepper

MARINADE:
50 g/2 oz raisins
65 g/2½ oz flaked almonds
1 tablespoon clear honey
2 garlic cloves, peeled
5 cm/2 inch piece fresh root ginger, peeled
and chopped
½ teaspoon cardamom pods
½ teaspoon cumin seeds
1 teaspoon turmeric
150 ml/5 fl oz yoghurt
120 ml/4 fl oz single cream

TO COOK THE CHICKEN:
¼ teaspoon saffron threads, soaked in 2
tablespoons boiling water for 10 minutes
50 g/2 oz butter, melted

Make diagonal slits in each chicken breast. Combine the lemon juice, salt and cayenne pepper, and rub the mixture all over the chicken, especially into the slits. Put the chicken into a large bowl and set aside for 30 minutes.

TO MAKE THE MARINADE: put the raisins, almonds, honey, garlic and spices into a blender with 4 tablespoons of yoghurt, and blend to a smooth purée. Transfer to a bowl and beat in the remaining yoghurt and cream. Pour over the chicken, cover the bowl and chill in the refrigerator for 24 hours, turning occasionally.

Remove from the refrigerator and set aside at room temperature for 1 hour.

TO COOK THE CHICKEN: heat the oven to 200°C/400°F/Gas Mark 6. Put the chicken in a deep roasting pan, reserving the marinade. Combine the saffron mixture with the marinade and pour it over the chicken. Spoon a little of the melted butter over the top. Roast the chicken for ½ hour or until it is tender, basting frequently with the remaining melted butter and the liquid in the roasting pan. If there is not enough marinade, add a small quantity of water.

TO SERVE: transfer the chicken to a warmed serving dish. Spoon the pan juices over the chicken.

SPINACH RICE

COOKING LIQUID:
575 ml/19 fl oz beef or veal stock
1 medium onion, peeled and quartered
4 cloves garlic, peeled
7 whole cloves
4 cardamom pods
2 teaspoons whole fennel seeds
1 teaspoon cumin seeds
1 teaspoon coriander seeds
stick of cinnamon
6 black peppercorns
1 bay leaf

SPINACH RICE:
375 g/13 oz Basmati rice
6 tablespoons vegetable oil
1 teaspoon garam masala (see page 89)
2 onions, peeled and chopped finely
2×227 g/8 oz packets frozen leaf spinach,
thawed and squeezed dry

GARNISH:
onion rings, deep-fried in oil or ghee

TO PREPARE THE COOKING LIQUID: pour the stock into a heavy-bottomed saucepan. Wrap the remaining cooking liquid ingredients into a piece of muslin, firmly knotted or tied with string, and add to the pan. Bring to the boil, reduce the heat, cover and simmer for 30 minutes. Lift out the muslin bag and squeeze it over the pan to extract as much flavoured liquid as possible. Measure the liquid and top it up with water if necessary to make 575 ml/19 fl oz. Leave to cool.

TO COOK THE RICE: wash the rice 3 times in cold water. Place it in a large heavy-bottomed saucepan and pour over the cold stock. Bring to the boil. Cover, reduce the heat and simmer for 25 minutes. Turn off the heat but leave the saucepan covered.

TO PREPARE THE SPINACH RICE: heat the oil in a heavy saucepan, add the garam masala and sauté for 5 minutes. Reduce the heat, add the chopped onions, and cook until soft but not browned. Add the spinach and stir to combine with the onions. Heat through. Fold the onion and spinach mixture into the hot rice.

TO SERVE: place in a serving bowl and garnish with crisply fried onion rings.

GARAM MASALA

3 tablespoons black peppercorns, ground
1 tablespoon ground cumin
1 teaspoon ground cinnamon
2 teaspoons ground cardamom
3 tablespoons ground coriander
1 teaspoon ground cloves
1½ teaspoons ground mace
½ teaspoon grated nutmeg

In a bowl, combine all the ingredients thoroughly. Transfer to a tightly covered container and store in a cool dry place.

CUCUMBER RAITA

(Cucumber and Yoghurt Salad)

600 ml/1 pint plain yoghurt
½ cucumber, washed and diced
4 spring onions, chopped finely
salt
pepper
¼ teaspoon paprika

Beat the yoghurt in a bowl until it is smooth, then beat in the cucumber and spring onions. Season to taste. Spoon into a serving bowl, cover and chill in the refrigerator for 1 hour. Sprinkle with paprika just before serving.

Aromatic Spinach Rice accompanies tender Spiced Almond Chicken.

MENU FOR FOUR

Beetroot consommé

BEEF STROGANOFF WITH BUTTERED HERBED RICE

Sweet cream cheese with almonds and sultanas

▼

Wine: French or Australian Hermitage

BOEUF STROGANOFF

100 g/4 oz butter
1 small onion, peeled and chopped
finely
100-175 g/4-6 oz button mushrooms,
sliced finely
salt
freshly ground black pepper
325 ml/11 fl oz soured cream
625 g/1¼ lb fillet steak, beaten thin and
cut into 5 mm/¼ inch strips

Melt 50 g/2 oz of the butter in a small heavy-bottomed saucepan over a moderate heat. Add the onion and fry gently until transparent. Add the mushrooms and cook, stirring from time to time, for 3-4 minutes. Season well. Reduce the heat and blend in the soured cream. Take care that the cream does not boil.

In a frying pan set over a high heat melt the remaining butter and cook the strips of beef quickly until nicely browned all over. Combine the meat with the sauce and serve immediately.

BUTTERED HERBED RICE

225 g/8 oz long-grain rice, cooked
75 g/3 oz butter
salt and freshly ground black pepper
2 tablespoons freshly chopped mixed
herbs, such as parsley, lemon thyme,
rosemary, marjoram

Melt the butter in a heavy saucepan over a moderate heat. Stir in the cooked and drained rice, salt and pepper, and mix it well to coat the grains with butter. Add the chopped herbs and serve immediately.

MENU FOR SIX

Seafood brochettes

BREAST OF CHICKEN AVOCADO WILD RICE IRENE

Profiteroles

▼

Wine: French white Burgundy

BREAST OF CHICKEN AVOCADO

3 whole chicken breasts, skin removed
2 tablespoons melted butter
2 tablespoons oil
salt
freshly ground black pepper

TOMATO COULIS:
6 large ripe tomatoes, peeled, seeded and
chopped finely
1 tablespoon olive oil
1 leek, white part only, chopped finely
12-20 basil leaves, chopped finely
salt
freshly ground white pepper

AVOCADO CREAM:
2 tablespoons brandy
6 spring onions, white part and a little of
the green, chopped finely
juice of 1 lemon
2 large ripe avocados, peeled and stoned
2 teaspoons salt
½ teaspoon white pepper
300 ml/½ pint single cream
milk, if needed

TO MAKE THE TOMATO COULIS: blend the tomatoes to a pulp in a food processor or push them through a sieve. Heat the olive oil in a small heavy saucepan and fry the leek gently until soft and thoroughly cooked, but do not let it take colour. Add the tomato and basil and season to taste. Continue to cook, stirring occasionally, until the sauce is thick and smooth. Remove from the heat and set aside.

TO MAKE THE AVOCADO CREAM: heat and flame the brandy. Place the spring onions in a blender with the brandy and lemon juice and run on a low speed until smooth. Add the avocado flesh, season well and blend again, slowly adding the cream, to make a thick sauce. Alternatively, pound the onions with the flamed brandy and lemon juice in a mortar to make a smooth paste. Transfer to a mixing bowl. Season well. Place a strainer over the bowl and press the avocado flesh through to make a purée. Beat the onions and avocado together and add the cream with one hand while stirring with the other. If the sauce is too thick, add a little milk. Transfer the mixture to a saucepan.

TO COOK THE CHICKEN: with a sharp knife, take the chicken breasts off the bone, to give 6 individual pieces. Heat the melted butter and oil in a heavy-bottomed frying pan. Add the chicken breasts, place the lid on the pan and cook over a very low heat. Check in about 3 minutes. When the breasts turn white on the edges, turn them over and cook for a further few minutes (approximately 3). Be careful not to overcook. Remove from the pan immediately, season and keep warm.

TO SERVE: heat the sauces separately. Pour some tomato coulis on individual warmed plates. Place a chicken breast on top and spoon the avocado cream over the chicken.

WILD RICE IRENE

1.2 litres/2 pints water
1 teaspoon salt
350 g/12 oz wild rice
1×230 g/8oz can water chestnuts, sliced
2 tablespoons chopped chives
freshly ground black pepper

Place the water in a large saucepan over a high heat. When the water is at a full boil, add the salt and rice, reduce the heat, cover the pan and simmer for about 45 minutes or until most of the liquid is absorbed. Drain if necessary, add the water chestnuts, chives and pepper to taste, and transfer to a warmed platter to serve.

Breast of Chicken Avocado, served with Wild Rice Irene, combines colours with style.

SON-IN-LAW EGGS

7 eggs, hard-boiled and shelled
vegetable oil for deep frying

SAUCE:
2 cloves garlic, peeled and crushed
1 tablespoon vegetable oil
2-3 sliced chillies, according to size
120 ml/4 fl oz liquid tamarind
  concentrate mixed with 120 ml/4 fl oz
  water
75 g/3 oz palm sugar or brown sugar
4 tablespoons nam pla (fish sauce)
2 tablespoons ready-fried red onions
  (available in packets from Asian stores)

Heat enough oil in a wok or deep fryer to fry the 7 eggs. Fry the eggs until golden in colour: this may take a little more time than you anticipate. Remove the eggs with a slotted spoon and drain on a paper towel.
TO MAKE THE SAUCE: in a heavy frying pan, fry the garlic in the oil, add the chillies, tamarind water, sugar, nam pla, and the onions. Allow the sauce to simmer, stirring occasionally, until it thickens.
TO SERVE: cut the eggs in half with a sharp knife and arrange on a platter. Pour the sauce over the eggs and serve immediately.

STIR-FRIED THAI NOODLES

225 g/8 oz flat rice noodles
5 tablespoons vegetable oil
1 large clove garlic, peeled and crushed
450 g/1lb uncooked prawns, peeled and
  cleaned
1 tablespoon soy sauce
3 tablespoons chopped preserved radish
2 tablespoons nam pla (fish sauce)
1½ tablespoons white vinegar
1 tablespoon palm sugar or brown sugar
200 g/7 oz bean sprouts
6 spring onions, in 5 cm/2 inch lengths

GARNISH:
100 g/4 oz roasted peanuts, chopped
coarsely ground black pepper

Place the noodles in a large bowl. Pour over enough hot water to cover them by 5 cm/2 inches and leave them to soak. When they have softened, drain and set aside.

Place a wok or large frying pan over a moderate heat. When it is warm, pour in the oil, add the garlic and cook it, stirring gently, for 2-3 minutes. Add the prawns and cook for 2 more minutes. Increase the heat and add the noodles, soy sauce, radish, nam pla, vinegar, sugar and 1 tablespoon of hot water. Cook for 1 minute, stirring constantly. Finally add the bean sprouts and spring onions. Stir-fry the mixture for 2 minutes more. Transfer to a warmed serving dish, garnish with peanuts and a sprinkling of pepper and serve immediately.

CURRY STEAMED RICE WITH CUCUMBER RELISH

225 g/8 oz long-grain rice
4 cloves garlic, peeled and chopped finely
2 tablespoons freshly grated ginger
3 tablespoons soy sauce
250 ml/8 fl oz vegetable oil
1½ tablespoons curry powder
450 g/1 lb fillet of beef, sliced thinly
75 g/3 oz mushrooms, sliced
2 dried lime leaves
½ cinnamon stick
1 tablespoon ready-fried red onions
350-500 ml/12-18 fl oz chicken stock
3 tomatoes, quartered

CUCUMBER RELISH:
120 ml/4 fl oz vinegar
65 g/2½ oz sugar
1 tablespoon salt
150 g/5 oz small thin slices cucumber
2 tablespoons thin slices red onion
2 chillies, seeded and sliced very thinly
5-6 coriander leaves

Wash the rice and drain it well. With a pestle and mortar or in a small bowl with a wooden spoon pound together the garlic, ginger and soy sauce to form a paste. Heat the oil, add the paste and cook for 3-4 minutes, stirring well. Add the curry powder, sliced beef, rice, mushrooms, lime leaves, cinnamon stick and red onions. Add the chicken stock gradually, 120 ml/4 fl oz at a time, as the rice cooks (see Risotto on page 15) and when almost ready, fork in the tomatoes.
TO MAKE THE CUCUMBER RELISH: combine the vinegar with the sugar and salt in a mixing bowl. Add the cucumber, onion and chillies. Reserving 1 or 2 coriander leaves for a garnish, chop the rest and add to the relish.
TO SERVE: transfer the rice mixture to a warmed bowl, and garnish the relish with the reserved coriander leaves.

THAI MUSLIM CURRY

PASTE:

1½ tablespoons vegetable oil
7 cloves garlic, peeled and chopped finely
1 large red onion, peeled and chopped
  finely
5 red chillies, deseeded and shredded
  finely
2 teaspoons dried laos
1 stalk lemon grass, chopped finely
½ teaspoon ground cloves
1 teaspoon ground cinnamon
6 cardamom seeds
½ teaspoon ground nutmeg
4 bay leaves, shredded
½ teaspoon blachan (shrimp paste)
½ teaspoon salt

CURRY:

2 kg/4 lb braising steak, cut in
  2.5 cm/1 inch cubes
120 ml/4 fl oz vegetable oil
1 litre/1¾ pints coconut cream
100 g/4 oz salted roasted peanuts
120 ml/4 fl oz nam pla (fish sauce)
1 stick cinnamon
seeds from 4 cardamom pods
1 tablespoon liquid tamarind concentrate
juice of 2 limes
2 tablespoons palm sugar or brown sugar
6 dried lime leaves

TO MAKE THE PASTE: heat 1 tablespoon of vegetable oil in a medium frying pan over a moderate heat. Add the garlic and onion and cook until the onion is soft and transparent. Remove and set aside. Into the pan place all the remaining ingredients except the blachan and salt. Add a little more oil if necessary and cook, stirring, for 5 minutes. Return the onions and garlic to the pan and combine well. Then remove the pan from the heat and stir in the blachan. Season with salt to taste.

TO MAKE THE CURRY: place the meat in a deep bowl. Add the paste and stir well to coat the pieces of meat thoroughly. Cover with a clean tea towel and leave for 1 hour for the meat to absorb the flavour. Heat the oil in a large frying pan over a medium heat and fry the coated meat until golden brown all over. Stir in the coconut cream and peanuts and continue to cook until the meat is almost tender. Transfer the meat and sauce to a deep saucepan. Add the nam pla, cinnamon stick and cardamom seeds and simmer over a gentle heat until the meat is quite tender. Stir in the tamarind concentrate, lime juice, sugar and lime leaves, cover the pan and cook for a further 15 minutes.

Clockwise from centre left: Son-in-Law Eggs, Thai Muslim Curry, a cabbage salad, Stir-fried Thai Noodles, Curry-Steamed Rice and relishes.

MENU FOR EIGHT

Liver pâté on toast with cornichons and watercress

ARMENIAN LAMB WITH RICE PILAF

Purée of guavas with sliced banana and passionfruit sauce

▼

Wine: Spanish red Rioja

ARMENIAN LAMB

1 tablespoon oil
25 g/1 oz butter
1.5 kg/3 lb trimmed lamb leg steaks, cut in
  5 cm/2 inch squares
3 onions, peeled and sliced
2 cloves garlic, peeled and crushed
1-2 tablespoons plain flour
6 teaspoons cumin
3 teaspoons allspice
2 tablespoons tomato purée
1×425 g/15 oz can beef consommé and
  ½ can water
salt and freshly ground black pepper

Heat the oven to 190°C/375°F/Gas Mark 5.

Heat the oil and butter in a frying pan and brown the meat a few pieces at a time. Remove the meat and set aside. Add the onions and garlic to the pan and cook for 5 minutes. Dust in the flour and spices, stir in the tomato purée, consommé and water.

Place the meat in a casserole, add the sauce, taste for salt and pepper, cover and cook for 1-1½ hours, adding more water if necessary. Stir once or twice during cooking.

Rice Pilaf is an appropriate accompaniment for Armenian Lamb.

RICE PILAF

75 g/3 oz butter
2 small onions, peeled and chopped finely
375 g/13 oz long-grain rice
900 ml/1½ pints chicken stock made with
  6 chicken stock cubes
salt
freshly ground black pepper
175 g/6 oz dates, stoned and cut in slivers
175 g/6 oz pistachio nuts, shelled and
  halved
chopped coriander
zest of 2 large limes, blanched

Melt the butter in a large heavy saucepan, add the onion and fry until soft but not brown. Add the rice and cook until translu-cent. Pour on the hot stock, season and, stirring all the time, bring to the boil. Cover the saucepan, reduce the heat and cook for 30 minutes or until cooked. When testing the rice, stir with a fork to avoid breaking up the grains. Add extra butter or stock if necessary. When cooked, gently stir in the dates, nuts, coriander and lime zest.

INDEX

Numbers in **bold** indicate pictures